Feel Good and Watch What Happens
By Anthea Morphitis

Anthea Morphitis

Feel Good and Watch What Happens

An Imprint of YUSA LTd

www.YUSALIFE.com - *Connect@YUSAbundance.com* **609 Quayside Tower 252-260 Broad Street, Second Floor, Birmingham, United Kingdom, B1 2HF**

Feel Good and Watch What Happens

By Anthea Morphitis

All rights reserved. No part of this book may be duplicated or replicated in any manner whatsoever physically, digitally or by any other means nor stored in any information storage system without prior written consent from the publisher or Author directly, except in the case of quotations with proper reference embodied in critical articles or reviews. All quotations and references remain the intellectual property of the respective originators. All quotations and references are under fair use copyright principal. Interior Images & artwork referenced accordingly throughout the book.

Cover Art & Illustration provided by Wesley

Arch Published In England

ISBN - 978-0993085987

Copyright ©2014 YUSALIFE

Anthea Morphitis

Table of Contents

Foreword 4
Acknowledgements 6
Introduction 8
Chapter 1: Break-up of the Family 10
Chapter 2: Teenage Pregnancy 21
Chapter 3: Pregnant Again 27
Chapter 4: Feeling Lonely 35
Chapter 5: 'In Love' 39
Chapter 6: The "Secret" Step in the right direction 44
Chapter 7: Expecting the Worst 47
Chapter 8: Mind, Body & Soul 56
Chapter 9: Court Cases 62
Chapter 10: Two Steps Forward, One Step Back 70
Chapter 11 Becoming Homeless & The Turning point 76
Chapter 12: The Law of Attraction 81
Chapter 13: The Power of Now 87
Chapter 14: How We Feel is The Indicator to the experiences ahead 95
Chapter 15: Setting a New Point of Attraction 104
Chapter 16: Limiting Beliefs 112
Chapter 17: Is There a Limit for What I Can Manifest? 129
Chapter 18: Believing In My Ideas 139
Chapter 19: Faith 148
Chapter 20: Relationships 151
Transition 155
Epilogue 157
About The Author 163

Foreword

I write this under the influence of pride for a friend above all and a client. Firstly, before my full awareness of Anthea's intention to embark on a journey to write a book detailing her personal life and realisations. I've always been conscious from our first contact of the natural ability Anthea possess to positivity and to inspire the people she encounters. For that, I have unconditional respect for wherever present.

I'm sure the general response given to so-called coincidences is globally known, and you probably say it yourself "everything happens for a reason."

I don't give thought to coincidence only synchronicities and that we live in a universe malleable by the dominant thoughts generated by the self-pulling into your reality scenarios and people that match your thoughts. Having said that it's hard to determine who attracted who into who's life when I think about it. I met Anthea through someone who I was sharing some of my research with, and he suggested I speak with Anthea as we were both showing symptoms of socially abnormal happiness and positivity. From our first conversation, I had a feeling that I'd met someone who's switched on in a similar way to myself. After many months of discussions on Skype, Anthea got involved with one of our early ventures and prepared content around the law of attraction which was received very well by our small community at the time. Unfortunately, the contact between Anthea and me had petered out, and we lost touch.

At the start of Summer 2014, I was working on publishing the YUSA Guide to Balance and was posting the progress on social media and getting great feedback and interest from all over the world. My business partner let me know that he had heard from Anthea and that she was in the final stages of completing her book, I instantly knew, before reconnecting with her, what was coming and exactly what was

Anthea Morphitis

going to unfold.

It brings me to this point where I have the honour of the task of presenting this semi-biographic depiction of an awakening to the power of the universe. This book is not only a very personal insight into the hardships that can be experienced in life but also empirical evidence of the law of attractions existence. I find myself like many others to be somewhat of an advocate of the law of attraction. I would recommend this title to people of all backgrounds wanting to understand and see how this universal law can be applied in times where there does not seem to be a light at the end of the tunnel. The book will serve as a handy companion and motivational tool for those directly experiencing the problems one can encounter as a single parent and how to overcome the feeling of powerlessness to create a brighter outcome.

Conclusively I welcome you to the debut title written by Anthea Morphitis*: Feel Good And Watch What Happens*, I only hope you enjoy reading it as much I have enjoyed working on it.

Axsal Johnson

Anthea Morphitis

Acknowledgements

Firstly, I would like to thank you; my reader, for picking up this book and wanting to know what will happen when you feel good. I, as the author, am happy as this means you are ready to live the best feeling life in each living moment, experiencing the best of life.

Always Remember Life is a Gift

I thank my parents for bringing me into this world for allowing me to live this precious life. To my Mum, you are an angel; thank you for being there every step of the way and Thank you, for believing in me when others didn't, sticking up for me when people were putting me down and for being a rock to my children and me when I felt I couldn't do it anymore. You have been the greatest. Love you, Mum.

I thank Abraham Hicks (Ester). Words can't describe how much I appreciate Abraham and her team. Listening, watching and reading all her material has changed my life, given me all the hope, belief and expectations that everybody deserves to have. I now have the opportunity to share my knowledge and understanding, giving you my readers an insight into a journey to feeling good.

I also thank Axsal from the YUSALIFE Team, for his friendship, willingness to give his time so generously and having the faith and belief in my work.

Thank you to Wesley Arch for his time, energy and understanding of creating the book cover and fantastic Logo your work is phenomenal and very much appreciated.

Anthea Morphitis

Feel Good and Watch What Happens

A massive thank you goes out to all my amazing friends who have been through my journey with me words can't describe how much I appreciate you all.

Last but not least, I want to thank my two amazing children for supporting me, loving me regardless of my flaws and loving me unconditionally. You two are my rocks, I love you both so much and am very proud of you both. You have given me the strength and courage to go on when I felt I could no longer live another day. You have brightened my days and nights by just being who you are. You have inspired me to take control, to love, to live life to the fullest and to follow my bliss. You are my angels. I am so proud to have you both as my children. Thank you for choosing me to be your mother. Love you always xxx.

Anthea Morphitis

Introduction

Feel Good and Watch What Happens is a semi-autobiography and semi self-help book written to show the importance of believing that anything is possible, despite where you stand in life right now.

Happiness is the key to life and will guide you to the fulfilment of your passions, dreams and desires.

I was inspired to write a book from a young age. From the age of 12 friends would often say, "Anthea, you should write a book about your life. I believe the reason my friends would tell me to write a book is because of the many bold experiences my life presented to me year after year.

Before March 2012, I never felt the urge or inspiration to start writing. However, early in 2012, the urges started. I felt like I was ready. I have now made a conscious and brave decision to share my life journey so far, to use myself as an example of the benefits gained while studying the Law of Attraction.

My goal is to show how putting my understandings of The Law of Attraction into action and becoming happy has led my life to change for the better. Allowing my dreams and aspirations of becoming an author, coach and inspirational speaker be realised.

As you read, you will get to know what type of journey I have been on thus far and why I reached a point in my life where I decided enough was enough and began to educate myself on The Law of Attraction, practising self-development, breaking cycles to re-create new experiences

I now love to teach and love to know that I have inspired. My most incredible feeling comes from knowing that my high energy, vibes and smile rub off on others, and brings a new positive thought about

Anthea Morphitis

Feel Good and Watch What Happens

life. I have come to believe; we create our reality, and we hold power to do so within us!

I love the fact that, after having a conversation with someone, the person walks away feeling good about who they are and grow a sense of belief in his or her self. The fact that that person inspires me, and I am also able to learn so much about myself and others through these conversations gives me great satisfaction! I love to see others prosper, getting to know who they are, understanding their natural wellbeing and most importantly, being part of their breakthroughs to happiness!

I am sharing my knowledge and have faith; it will reach people around the world. I hope to create awareness of the power of self-love and forgiveness. Inspiring happiness, a positive mindset and raising awareness that we have full control of every situation in our life experiences right now. My message: Every circumstance created is due to the focus and attention on that subject.

I intend that anyone who reads this will gain a better understanding of who we are, how energy flows through us, and how important, unique and worthy we are to this world.

This book is now in your hands to help you understand and believe in the power you hold, and with faith and belief, you can be, do or have anything your heart desires. To also give my personal touch to the world, share my journey as a single parent and the technics I use to overcome adversity. Sharing the power of thoughts and emotions and sharing quotes that inspire me from others

Anthea Morphitis

Chapter 1: Break-up of the Family

"Feel good and watch what happens!" Haha. If you had said that to me six years ago, I would have looked at you first, ready to beat you up and secondly, I would have said, "What!! Can you not see what is happening in my life right now? My life is crap! How could you expect me to feel good?"

Me at Two Years Old

Well, anything is possible, as I have found out first-hand. My life always appeared to be full of adverse situations. When I was growing up, I never understood why, primarily as I was known as "happy go lucky". I have always gone through life with a smile, but hurting deep within, not wanting to show and express to anyone how I felt, I would often just gracefully smile!

Anthea Morphitis

Feel Good and Watch What Happens

My family and I lived in a lovely comfortable three-bedroom house in North London, surrounded by everything a child would want. We had a beautiful park at the back of the garden and were friends with all our neighbours. It was, and still is, a mini Cyprus in Palmer's Green, North London. All the neighbours would come round to each other's houses. We would have friends and family around on weekends, or there would be some kind of family event like a birthday, wedding or christening taking place. It was nice to be surrounded by so many loved ones, as this is where, as children; we found comfort and contentment, as it was a whole different story behind closed doors!

My mum was in an unhappy relationship with my dad due to their issues, and I believe she was unhappy throughout their marriage. It affected my brother and me as children and created an unbearable atmosphere. We all wanted out, as not one of us enjoyed being at home. Even as beautiful as our surroundings were, we didn't want to be there, I remember Mum going on driving lessons. I would sit by the front door for the whole duration, crying my eyes out until she got home. I never really had a positive relationship and a bond with my dad.

My Mum was the owner of a clothes factory. We loved going there on the weekends, (many Greek Cypriots were part of the rag trade in the 80s, and other family members also worked there); it was a fun place to be. While working, mum fell in love with another man who also happened to be in an unhappy marriage, and so they found comfort in each other. However, a considerable problem stood in the way—the man she had fallen in love with was Turkish Cypriot!

Let me explain: Before 1974, the Greeks and Turks lived on the island together in peace and harmony until Turkey Invaded Cyprus, creating a war. Unfortunately, People forced out of their homes, and friends became enemies.

Turkey took over the island, splitting the Island in two, Greek

Anthea Morphitis

Feel Good and Watch What Happens

Cypriots in the South and Turkish Cypriots in the North and causing massive conflict between the Greek and Turkish Community. To the point that it was utterly unacceptable to be seen with a Turkish person, never mind leaving your Greek Cypriot husband for one! My mum was willing to lose everything just to find happiness for us all.

So, with the impression our lives were filled with new, exciting and happy experiences, we left the family home behind.

Then, at the tender age of 7, my whole world changed! The excitement very quickly turned to despair—my life was about to become a roller coaster of emotions. The action led to Mum and dad divorcing eventually, and our entire family disowning us! My dad had people follow us daily to and from school photographing and filming to send evidence to our family in Cyprus that my mum was with a 'Turk'!! Crazy, but true. This was a crazy time for me: adults seemed weird, and I just thought everyone was mad.

Anthea Morphitis

Feel Good and Watch What Happens

Above is a photograph of my brother and I aged around six and nine years old.

From the split onwards, we moved from one place to another, the first place being a one-room hostel with my mum, brother and now stepdad. I remember arriving, looking around in despair and not understanding what was happening. I still remember the damp smell and the feeling of confusion being so strong within me. Where were my dolls? Where were my clothes? Where was my lovely comfortable bedroom?

We'd had to leave the family home so suddenly that we went with just the clothes on our backs. All of a sudden, I felt so alone. I had so many questions about the new experiences but had no one to ask. I found this very difficult to deal with, both mentally and emotionally,

Anthea Morphitis

Feel Good and Watch What Happens

especially as I was only 7. My mum thought she had left behind her unhappy marriage, but little did she know, as time unfolded, she had just walked straight into another one!

Following my parents' divorce, we had to go to court. I remember a lady asking me to draw a picture, one of myself with my mum, brother and stepdad and another of me, my brother and dad. The one I drew of myself with my mum and co. was with smiles and the one with my dad was with sad faces. The reason for this was that every time I went to my dad's, he would shout and call my mum every name under the sun.

Therefore, I would often dread going to see him, as I knew what I would hear and it would hurt hearing such negative words about my mum, despite what was going on in our' new lives'. As I got older, contact with my dad became less. At the age of 11, I chose not to go and see him anymore due to the constant negative attitude and interrogation to learn about my mum.

When I was 9, we moved into a three-bedroom house, which was the first time we felt settled in two years, I had moved schools and lost contact with most of my friends I had grown up with, but on the upside, the school was only a fifteen-minute walk and just a minute stroll into the Town Centre. From my first day at my new school, I met some great people and still hold a friendship with them today. During this time, is when I was really able to settle and start socialising again and building new friendships and finally began to feel happy again.

While living there, I became very independent, at the age of 11, a friend and I who lived a few doors away, started our own car wash business; this gave me the freedom to buy things that I wanted as we had a couple of blocks of offices on our road and most employees that

worked there had become our customers, which in turn gave me a fantastic feeling as I no longer had to ask my mum for money. The only

Anthea Morphitis

Feel Good and Watch What Happens

issue with this was, I was using my surroundings to determine my happiness!!

When I was 12, we were on the move again. This time, we moved to a rough estate, where I spent most of my teenage years. Arriving there was extremely daunting! Living on an estate opened my eyes to a different way of life that I did not particularly like but had to accept. I had to work with what was around me and try to fit in.

I was offered to try cannabis at the age of 15 and liked the high it gave me and used it as a mental and emotional escape route from life daily.

I never touched any other types of drug, even though many people around me did. I always used to tell myself that if I took anything other than cannabis, I would drop dead, and I turned this into a belief for myself, so I never did do any other drugs, which was very good. I tried alcohol for the first time when I was 12 and had got myself so drunk that I was extremely sick and unwell; to be fair I appreciate the fact that I had done that as I very rarely touch alcohol due to that experience. I had also got myself arrested for silly things and was starting to turn into a rebel.

Being in this environment quickly changed my mindset from abundance to not enough, from stability to instability, from worthy to unworthy. Without even knowing it, these become my new beliefs about me, my words and actions mirrored these beliefs.

Eventually, I began to understand how to be around certain people knowing how to take myself away from the situations that I perceived to be 'bad" while staying neutral to everyone to avoid conflict.

However, I must say a considerable amount of my best memories are from that estate and blessed with the most amazing friends that again are still in my life today. I found an escape from what I felt at the time to be 'bad" family life in my very dear neighbour, who became a

Anthea Morphitis

Feel Good and Watch What Happens

mother figure to me and who helped me understand the value of family and friends again. She was there for me whenever I needed to confide in someone, and her family welcomed me like I was one of their own! I truly appreciated the love.

When a teenage girl has to deal with so many changes and issues all at one time, sometimes one escape is not enough, hence why I also found comfort in another friends mum, who would allow me to be at her home during school hours and thought she was the best mother anyone could ask. We laugh and joke about it now the fact that I would play truant at her home; she kept my spirits high by her crazy personality, and till this day, we have a fantastic relationship.

I was so angry with my mother and myself that had I known what I know now; I would have appreciated the fact that I had a mother who loves me unconditionally, a roof over my head and home-cooked food on the table every day. However, I could not see this; caught up in my anger. Many of us experience this, I believe, especially as teenagers. We continuously search for more, which is fine as long as we appreciate what is in our face here and now. Life will always inspire us to more; I believe there is never a moment in time when we are not asking for something; this is the beauty of life.

I did not like school hence why I spent most of my school years 'bunking', as I felt misunderstood by the teachers and felt segregated as I had to move schools a few times.

I could not stand being told what to do, and had an attitude of: *"Who are you to tell me what I can and can't do!?"* I didn't understand this type of discipline as was not practised at home, deemed 'too much to handle' by my mum, stepdad and teachers.

When I did attend school, I was always on school report and excluded on a few occasions. I still had the question of: *"Why and how can others have the right over me!?"* I was known as a 'troubled teenager', and I

Anthea Morphitis

Feel Good and Watch What Happens

certainly lived up to that. My mindset was that I was born alone and found my way out alone; I was born naked, with nothing attached to me, so I couldn't understand what gave teachers or anyone else the right to say what I had done was right or wrong, good or bad. I felt like that, as it seemed there was no one ever to help me, but there was always someone to criticise me, and no one was taking time out to find out who I was and what was going on in my life due to what I was continually attracting in life, how I felt about myself. As my new belief goes, we attract to ourselves what we are thinking and feeling.

Had I known this at the time, I wouldn't have needed others' approval or disapproval to know my worthiness.

I never really understood what the point was in lessons like History and Religion, as I had no interest in these subjects at the time and often questioned the teachers regarding what I would use this knowledge. Their response would usually be, "Get out of my classroom." Even today, I still don't understand why children learn certain subjects if they have no interest in them!

At one of my secondary schools, something happened that I never expected ever to happen, on my return after a Christmas break, a new girl had started and had become popular very quickly. She found out that I was one of the popular girls and somehow turned most of the school against me. Rumours started, becoming severe as I had received death threats. Terrified for my life, I turned to the headteacher, only to get told to get out of the office! Hard for me to get my head around, I didn't know which way to turn, especially as I travelled to and from school via public transport, and it was only a couple of months previously that someone got stabbed from the same school by the same crowd of people. With no support from the teachers, I played truant for several months and eventually expelled from school. I was fortunate not to live in that area anymore, and no one knew where I lived, so I happily left and found a school close by where I could start

Anthea Morphitis

Feel Good and Watch What Happens

again, well there was only one school in my local area that accepted me, due to my school report and the picture painted of me. This particular school happily gave students with a `bad` school report a chance.

Changing schools and starting fresh at 14, I began to revisit my dad on the weekends, and everything seemed fine. We never actually spoke about why I stopped seeing him; however, my brother had told him and encouraged me to reconnect with my dad, and I appreciate that he did that now.

Parents are so precious; so many of us find faults in them, when, without our parents, we would not be here. They are on a journey, just like every person on this planet, there is no step by step guide on 'How to raise your children' day to day teaches you that, as I believe: words do not teach, life experience teaches.

If there is one thing that stood out about me, I always held a smile on my face; smiling was one of the main reasons teachers would be upset with me, kicking me out from my lessons at school. I just wanted to have fun; however, everything was so earnest in lessons. Come to think about it, so many of us take our lives so seriously and forget to smile and laugh. As I got older, a question I often heard," How do you keep smiling while in the middle of crazy situations?". People close to me always found it an inspiration that I kept a smile; however, I knew in my heart of hearts that life is supposed to be fun and just wanted to live a happy life.

As a young child with a sharp mind, I always knew in my heart what was right, however constantly told I was wrong, it confused me.

The confusion was part of the reason I rebelled as a teenager, I also have a very crazy and outgoing personality, and I felt like school was a punishment to all kids. I wished more choices were offered rather than just being told what to do.

Anthea Morphitis

Feel Good and Watch What Happens

I often felt unloved, as I thought my mum had a new family: her husband and my little sister, who was born when I was 10. I would do things for attention, but would be told, "If you don't like living here, then go to your dad's!!" I would run away, just to let my mum know I was hurting. I wasn't happy and had a problem with my stepdad. My mum was never the type to discipline; she is a very soft-hearted woman and just wants to please. She wouldn't say boo to a goose; she is a much-loved woman, and I would often want to shake her to make her take some kind of control of her life. Any time my stepdad would try to say anything to me, my response would be, "You're not my dad!" I now know that was not the way to speak to someone who provided a home for us.

My experience has taught me, I now understand what my mum has gone through, and I appreciate, love and adore her as a person.

When you're a kid, you just don't get any of it, and I would have done anything I could to try and let her know that I still existed and believe or not, the only thing I didn't do was communicate how I felt! None of it had anything to do with my family: it was all to do with the way I felt about myself and the perception I held on what I thought others felt about me. Hence, life often felt like crap.

Mum is on a journey of her own, which I now understand, and despite the past, my mum is an amazing mother, woman, sister, auntie and grandmother. She hugs, kisses and tells my children every day that she loves them and we have a very loving relationship now because I no longer blame her or others for the way I am feeling about myself and others. I love the way my children love and adore her; they cannot go a day without speaking to her, and that alone makes my heart sing.

I was, if you like, a 'street kid'. There was nothing that could keep me at home. I just loved to be outside roaming. I just wanted to explore, have fun, be mischievous. At the age of 10, I would get on London transport and get myself lost, only so that I could find my way home

Anthea Morphitis

Feel Good and Watch What Happens

again. I loved it. Just after starting my new school around the age of 14, I met my perfect match to play truant with, she was in the year above me but was very much my mirror. We would wear a pair of leggings under our school skirt and a top under our shirts, signing in at our morning register at school, and the second the bell would go for lessons, we would run out of school, taking our school uniform off while running and jump on the first available bus. We would travel into Central London from North London and walk around for hours, or travel to South London where my friend's cousins lived, hanging out in the local snooker club. We had a lot of fun and continued to do this for a good three months until caught out, and unfortunately family barred us from being friends and hanging out together out of school hours.

I never took well to rules and school environment as I felt my freedom taken away from me. Hence, why I believe I developed a pretty bad attitude as I went through my teenage years. There were all these rules at school, and I would even speak to my friends in ways I would never dream of now, through my frustration. I would smoke cannabis' daily, which made my attitude worse, and at some points, I just didn't want to live!!

Through these experiences of emotions and situations, I developed feelings of self-doubt, fear and unworthiness, which affected my behaviour and habits of my thoughts about me and others. I was unaware of what I was attracting to myself by allowing myself to think and feel that way!

Anthea Morphitis

Chapter 2: Teenage Pregnancy

I attended college for a year and studied business studies. At that time, my real passion was to get into the travel industry. Still, I did not have the confidence and belief in myself to do it because of the views, I picked up off adults, and decided it would be the way forward to attend college as I was advised to and would look good on my CV if I studied business studies, so I did. Isn't it amazing what we do to satisfy others? But the truth is: you can't stand on your head enough ways to please another. We all have these dreams and aspirations, only to be told by adults that it is not possible to achieve them and that we should do something 'normal'. What is 'normal, anyway?' I do not believe that anything is 'normal' each to their own, I say!

I started my first job with a major fast-food chain and worked my butt off until I had enough to see me through my driving lessons and to buy a car. My dad was an angel, helping me to achieve this. Once I reached that, my next goal was to save enough money to get myself to Cyprus to escape the everyday life that I had grown so tired of, so I took on a second job.

I worked and lived in Cyprus for about a year and had a great time. Within a couple of days, I met some new people; amongst them was a young man that I immediately connected with, We very soon began a relationship together. I couldn't believe it: after just a few days of being in Cyprus, I had already met new friends and the man of my dreams. We decided to move in together and progress our relationship; I couldn't believe it; I was living the fairy-tale dream (well, so I thought). The fairy-tale soon came to an end after a few months, when I found out that he was living a double life and he was already engaged to his pregnant fiancée.

Let's stop for a minute and look at what I was carrying around with me. Why did I think that by moving to another country everything would

Feel Good and Watch What Happens

work out? Because I had no inkling of an idea that I felt like crap inside and I had created all these unswerving beliefs within me. I thought I could just move and automatically start anew, not understanding that you take yourself with you, which includes emotions, thoughts and beliefs.

Anyway, with this knowledge, I was immediately out the door, with all my belongings. I spent about a month with my brother, who was living in Ayia Napa, Cyprus.

Ayia Napa is `Party Central` People fly from all over the world due to its party reputation. So in the perspective of others, I am Lucky to be partying every night! However, I still felt hurt and broken but suppressed my emotions by partying all night and sleeping all day. It was also helpful being with my brother as I felt safe and secure in his presence he introduced me to so many people that life seemed pretty sweet; however, I couldn't keep this up forever and soon decided to move back to London.

Within a week of being back in London, I landed a local job within a big company. I was quickly offered a better position further away, in an area called Reading, which is about an hour journey from North London and was offering better prospects and salary. I made the decision to move there and enjoyed my new role within the company; however, I did struggle to settle without friends and family and moved back to London within the year, commuting to work instead.

I soon grew tired of this and decided to have a re-think about my career. I found it challenging to stay in one place and just loved moving from place to place. I got bored quickly, and I always had to have something that stimulated me and something new to focus on, but I wasn't pursuing what I wanted. I worked in offices just because of money! Is this not what a large population of us does? Seek employment For the simple fact that it pays, which leads to placing passions and desires to the side, not having enough time, and when

Anthea Morphitis

having the time not having the inspiration to work towards making them happen and eventually suppressing them.

My genuine desire was to find a job that enabled me to travel; I loved the thought of travelling and getting paid to do so and the fact most of my family who lives in Cyprus had many connections in the local airport in some way or another. I returned to Cyprus in April 1999, intending to stay there and begin my new career with the travel industry. Just before leaving, I had applied for jobs on cruise ships; however, you have to be 21 to work on them, and I was 19 at the time.

I thought the easy option would be to move to Cyprus and once I turned 21, I could reapply.

My good friend happened to be getting married around the same time as I had moved there, I had attended her wedding who happened to be a mutual friend of my ex-partner with whom I had lived in Cyprus. So, I was not surprised to see that he was also at the wedding. By this point, he had split with his fiancée and was now a single man. We were sitting together at the same table and had a perfect time at the wedding. We found ourselves reconnecting with each other, just like the old times.

After a great night and some alcohol, we lost ourselves and spent the night together.

I was happy, as I still had a soft spot for him and thought we could make a go of our relationship again; however, I quickly realised that he hadn't changed and so we just remained friends. His brother and I were excellent friends; despite anything that had happened, we continued our friendship, and within a few weeks of being in Cyprus, I found out I was pregnant!!!

I couldn't believe my luck: how one night of passion had just outlined the rest of my life! I was 19 and pregnant in a different country and all

Anthea Morphitis

Feel Good and Watch What Happens

alone! What the hell was I going to do?

I had been staying with my uncle; anytime I would travel to Cyprus, my Uncle and Auntie would always welcome me with open arms. We all have a fantastic relationship; they also had two young children at the time that I love and adore, feeling much love and comfort being with my uncle's family. My uncle would be like a father figure to me when I was with him, he cared and loved me like I was one of his own, and I appreciated that.

Even though I had a great relationship with my family, the pregnancy was not something I felt I could tell them as they did not believe in pregnancy outside of wedlock.

My ex's brother was with me when I took the pregnancy test. His reaction was, "My brother is going to kill you." He made it clear to me that his brother would not take nicely to the news and suggested that I leave without telling him about the pregnancy. With that on my mind, I was scared and confused. I took the next flight out of the country, crying the whole way home, not knowing how I was going to do this alone.

I returned to London with this weight on my shoulders and no-one to confide in, I had no plans—just a bunch of emotions. I was scared out of my wits with my situation, but I knew there was nothing I could do but deal with it.

Two days after my return, I received a call from my uncle with some heart-breaking news. My little cousin, (my uncle's daughter), was diagnosed with Leukaemia, two days before her 5th birthday. Confused by the call, I was only with her a few days before that!

While staying with my uncle she had been showing symptoms of the flu and had been feeling unwell for a couple of weeks, but we did not think for one second that It would be that! We had grown close as we spent a lot of time together.

Anthea Morphitis

Feel Good and Watch What Happens

The day I was due to leave Cyprus, I had promised her I would return as soon as I could. She had gone out with her daddy, and together they bought me the most beautiful white gold necklace as an early birthday present, she had the biggest smile on her face and was so proud as she handed me this precious gift. I thanked her, told how much I loved her and gave her the biggest kiss and cuddle, saying our goodbyes.

I couldn't make up my mind, torn between staying in London and returning to Cyprus; however, the fact that I was pregnant stopped me from going as it didn't feel right to be there.

Scared to tell mum about the pregnancy as she was preparing to relocate to New York after my stepdad accepted an opportunity to work with my uncle.

I was scared that their reaction would be to have an abortion. I was entirely against abortions and knew that I would rather have a baby and deal with what was going to come from that than to put myself through the abortion process. I was very aware that my dream of working on cruise ships, for the time being, was over.

I waited until I was three months pregnant to tell anyone, as I knew once I hit the three-month stage, I had to see it through. Mum, stepdad and sister moved to America, on a trial basis and that's when I hit them with this bombshell. My brother and I moved into Mum's home until they made a firm decision about their move and was now felt all alone, in a vulnerable position. During this time, my little cousin admitted to the hospital, treated with chemotherapy; and was such a sad time for us all. Trying to get your head around something like that is not easy, I felt I couldn't speak to my uncle as I was pregnant and didn't know what to say.

I found a new job to try and occupy my mind and see me through this emotional time, and to be honest; it was the best decision I could have

Anthea Morphitis

Feel Good and Watch What Happens

made at that time. Meeting new people of the same age was a breath of fresh air. Everyone in the company was so supportive of me; we would often go out, and I loved working. It helped me deal with my pregnancy with ease and the reality of my little cousin having Leukaemia. I also grew to love the fact that I was going to be a mummy. Every day, my work colleagues would make such a fuss over me, and they were so excited to see how my belly was growing day by day and that alone made me feel like I was not alone.

What changed?? Meeting new people that knew nothing about my past, I felt free of all judgements and perspectives.

Mum and family decided to move back to London just before I had my baby; however, I believe this decision was made under the influences of other family members, as my stepdad was extremely reluctant to move back. I think that, in his eyes, he saw me as the cause that made him give up his life in America, just because I was, from his perspective, irresponsible and got myself into this situation. I tried to convince them to stay as I loved the fact that my mum had her sister in America whom she loved and missed dearly. But her decision was made, and they moved back.

Through my youth, I would try and move from place to place, thinking that if I got away from the situations, everything would be better. I did not realise that the problems were due to the emotions I felt within me, which created each experience. We really can't get away from ourselves! We can move 100 times, but as long as we have disbelief in ourselves and harbour anger, resentment and the habit of continually spewing the same story, we will continue to attract the same in life. I've now realised, changing my story, emotions and thoughts lead to changes in my life.

Anthea Morphitis

Chapter 3: Pregnant Again

My son was born four weeks early, in December 1999, after extraordinarily traumatic and life-threatening labour—again due to fear of giving birth. I finally got to meet my tiny little man, and what a feeling! It was the best I had experienced so far in my life! At this point, I decided to phone my ex to let him know that he was a father. His response was, "Whatever… he's not mine", and a little more was said, however, it's not suitable for this book, and no more contact made at this point.

Above a picture of my son and I at his Christening when he was five months old. His was so cute; I love him so much!

After putting down the phone, I felt shocked as I thought once the little man was born; his father would have some kind of interest. I cried for the rest of the day but knew I had to pull myself together as I had no control over him. I told him, and that's all I could do, mainly as he resided in Cyprus.

I continued to live at my mum's for the first five months of my baby's life, and all seemed nice and calm. It was a real blessing, as I had help at my fingertips and also enabled Mum and me to begin to build a relationship. Just as I had settled in and became accustomed to being a mum, my stepdad threw yet another bombshell at me; he was beginning to feel depression and found that having a baby around was not helping; it was causing him to feel worse. He then asked me to move out.

During this time, we received a call from my family in Cyprus that my little cousin lost her fight to Leukaemia and passed away around her 6th Birthday. I felt so guilty, I had a new life growing, and my little cousin was taken away from us at such a young age, she was my little angel.

I felt it was my fault as my belief at the time was when a baby is brought into this world another member of the family would leave. I believed, had I not had a baby she would still have her life. I walked around for days without saying a word; I was scared to speak to my uncle as I thought he would blame me; over time, our relationship became pretty much non-existent.

So, within a week, I was out on my own again, with nowhere to call home. I went to the local council for some help, and the council moved my baby and me into a bedsit, this was a massive shock to my system. I felt I had gone backwards in life and was re-creating the same situations that had happened when I was young. I had never dealt with the emotions, and unknowingly was still carrying them around within me. We had a small room and had to share a bathroom with

Five other residents, not an ideal situation with a baby, but I was thankful for having a roof over our heads and, in time, it gave me a sense of freedom, so eventually, I appreciated it.

"Where there is a will, there is a way."

We were there for around five months. My dad kindly offered to take my son and me for a holiday to Cyprus, to get away for a bit and this was hugely appreciated, as you can imagine. When we were out there, I happened to bump into my son's father for the first time since his birth. I must say that the universe works in mysterious ways, my ex happened to be doing building work on a house that was opposite the

Flat we were staying in, and an area I had never visited before. I couldn't believe what I was seeing.

I approached him without my baby, to speak with him. To my surprise, he seemed pleased to see me. We got talking about the whole situation, and I showed him a picture of his son. His response was, "Oh my god, I can't believe how much he looks like me! I can't deny he's my son." We arranged to meet up that night with some other friends and spent the entire night talking about everything, good and bad.

The next day, I introduced him to his son for the first time, which was quite emotional for both of us. We stayed in contact, on and off, for the duration of my holiday. The last time we spoke, he said that he would come and say goodbye to our son before we left. That day never came, so we made our way back to London with no love lost.

When we got back from Cyprus, I had an exciting letter waiting for me. It was from the council, stating we had a two-bedroom property to move into on the 3rd of December. I was so excited, especially as I knew my son's first birthday was soon approaching and will be celebrated at our new home. Finally, we had somewhere that we could settle and call home, with no one being able to tell us to leave.

I began a new relationship with a guy I'd met just before going to Cyprus with my dad. Things were looking up: a new home and a new man. My son was ten months old when we'd met, and this new man and his family were happy to accept the fact that I had a child from a previous relationship. We got on well, and he seemed very genuine.

I was so delighted that this person had walked into my life and was giving me the love and attention I craved. It wasn't long before he moved in with us; we were like a little 'family'. Then, just after a short time of being together, I found out I was pregnant again! Oh my god, how could this be? My world had just turned upside down and back to front.

I have never cried so much in my life. I went through every emotion known to man. I just wasn't ready for this again; nothing but negative emotions ran through my entire body every time I thought of the pregnancy; however, my partner was not fazed by it at all. Before I even had the chance to try and come to terms with what I had just discovered or to decide what I wanted to do, within the same 12 hours, my partner told his entire family, without even discussing it with me. Now if you know any Cypriots, you will know that our families are all related one way or another, which means people I didn't even know, knew about my pregnancy!

I was livid, for now, I had pressure coming from left, right and centre from him and his family. His family had also made it very clear to me that he was extremely unreliable; however, they would always be there for me. Already, they were telling me what I was going to do instead of asking me what I felt and wanted to do. They hounded me day and night. I had hit rock bottom and didn't know which way to turn to escape from their possessive behaviour! At this point, the relationship began to deteriorate; we didn't even have the chance to learn each other as people.

There was no real connection between us. I very quickly began to despise this person who decided to try and take over my thoughts and decisions with the help of his family. As I mentioned, his own family had warned me of his total lack of responsibility in everything. Already, they had created this whole negative picture of him, with this brought to my attention, this is how I now saw him and what I expected from him— just negativity and nothing else.

I finally decided to move forward with my pregnancy and give our relationship a chance. My daughter was born in June 2001; with

such joy of having a baby, unfortunately, I very quickly got to experience what his family was talking about, it turned out that his was a compulsive gambler and not afraid to become physical with a woman.

We made each other's life hell. We would always be at each other's throats. I would blame him, and he would blame me. The neighbours would regularly call the police due to all the commotion. I even had to call the police many times through fear for my life, as things got

Anthea Morphitis

Feel Good and Watch What Happens

extremely physical. All this and two young babies to care for; however, I was determined to make it work, just to satisfy others, and because I wanted my babies to have a father figure in their lives. I also didn't want to have everyone speaking negatively about me.

No matter what was happening the love I feel for my children is unconditional and eternal. Below is a photo of my daughter and me.

I had experienced stress previously in my life, but this situation took it to a whole new level, to the point where it caused me to suffer severely with my lower back. On one case, I remember waking up one morning to my baby crying and being in so much pain I could barely get myself out of bed. In an attempt to do so, I slowly pushed myself to get up; the pain was so bad I vomited, screaming for help, hoping a neighbour would hear me. I couldn't take it, and I dropped to my knees, passing out on my way down. I must have been out for just a few seconds, but it felt like forever. The baby's crying was getting louder. I knew I had to find the strength within me to get up, pull myself together and pick up my baby. I slowly crawled across the floor to my baby's cot, grabbing onto the handles, crying with pain. I heard my front door, and to my surprise, my mum walked in.

I don't think I had ever been so happy to see my mum. This pain carried on for the next couple of years. I went through times where I was bed-bound for weeks on end. My family were my rock; they were there for me every time and would take care of my children through these times.

I also experienced blackouts and nose bleeds pretty often, the blackouts become part of my daily life and knew exactly how to deal with them. Unfortunately, this is the results of stress; our body fights stress and causing physical pain and internal breakdown of the organs.

Despite our relationship breakdown, I did have a relationship with my partner's immediate and extended family. We didn't always

Anthea Morphitis

Feel Good and Watch What Happens

agree on situations and would argue saying harmful and unnecessary things to each other due to the high negative emotions we were all experiencing; however, we continued to spend time together. The family were there for my daughter, which was hugely appreciated.

Gambling is significant in the Greek community, and unfortunately, my ex-partner was addicted, leading to extra pressure on our relationship, which quickly turned to resentment towards him and total lack of respect. I no longer looked at him as a man, just as unwanted baggage.

I now know that it was because of the way I was thinking and feeling about everyone. My attention to the negative was what helped mould these situations into what they were. The constant negative energy that surrounded the case just kept on expanding; it was a vicious cycle, a cycle that no one understood how to break.

I hit points in my life where I wanted to give up; sometimes it was all too much, trying to be a mother to two young children and continually fighting the father and built pressure between my family and me because they couldn't understand why I wouldn't ask him to leave. It was all such a mess, and the pressure was immense. When I spoke to my parents, they would say, "Kick him out! No one likes him!" When I talked to the father's family, they would suggest that my daughter lived with them.

In my overall situation, I was continually attracting negative situations because of the way I was feeling. My focus was always on the problem and far from the solution.

I decided in January 2003 to ask him to leave. I believed that life would be so much better without being in a relationship with him and just living life without the extra stress that his life presented to my life. I thought it would get more comfortable as the pressure of the relationship was no longer in my home, but it just got worse, experiencing a whole bunch of adverse situations.

Anthea Morphitis

Feel Good and Watch What Happens

I spent all my time focusing on the things I did not like; I forgot that I was alive, breathing and had every limb in my body working in perfection. Despite having a roof over my head, two beautiful children and my mum close by, all I focused on was negative. I was blinded by it all, not aware that it was up to me to choose where I put my attention. If I had known different, then I could have chosen to give my focus and attention on the abundance of who I was and the things that surrounded me and appreciated every moment, instead of focusing on the problem and creating more negative feelings and circumstances.

Every problem has a solution, focus on the solution!

I was determined to work and earn my own money. I didn't like the thought of claiming from the authorities and the fact that I was young and loved and still love to shop. I wanted to receive more than what the government would provide. I loved taking my children out, I loved having a car, and I loved to do all the things you could do when there is a good flow of money.

I spent my life searching for guidance and acceptance from others when all along it's my job to accept me for who I am and use my intuition to guide me. I began to realise that I only needed myself to be happy, but the knowledge and realisation didn't stop the loneliness kicking in.

Anthea Morphitis

Chapter 4: Feeling Lonely

I can honestly hold my hands up and say, raising two young children without a partner can sometimes be one of the loneliest journeys anyone could imagine. While I would take my children to the park and love every second of it, I could not get away from the fact that I would have to watch all the other families running around, other children calling their mummy and daddy. All the time, in my mind, I did not believe that I could also have the same.

One child would run off while the other parent would watch the other. The mum would have the dad to speak to while having an ice-cream, and I would only have myself. I felt sorry for myself, and I would sit and dream that a man would be by my side, having the joy and pleasure of watching 'our' children running around.

I was seeing dads playing football with their sons, and it made my heart sing for the children but broke my heart for my child. I would take a football to the park and play football with them both.

In time, it did get more relaxed and better as they got older; as they began to understand and appreciate that I never just sat and moaned about it. I would keep us entertained for hours and often felt like our life was missing an essential piece of raising children and couldn't always help but get upset. I just wanted what the other mums had: someone to come home to, someone to take the pressure off me, someone to tell me it will be ok, and most of all, someone who could enjoy life as a family.

As it stands today, my son has met his dad around a handful of times in the past 13 years. I believe they will unite one day, and I hope they can build a strong positive relationship in time, especially now that my son has become a teenager. I feel it would be helpful for him to have his dad in his life, to grow a new relationship with each other, get to know one another and become friends.

Anthea Morphitis

Feel Good and Watch What Happens

Although I didn't hold the belief that we would experience having any of the father's support, have them come to the park, on holidays and so on, I'm blessed enough to have a mindset of fun and still experienced all this with my children regularly. We are a very outgoing family and love experiencing new things, and suppose I was determined to give my children what I would have liked to have experienced as a child.

My beautiful sister and I

I also have an amazing sister that has been there for me since my children were born; she has experienced a considerable amount of my life with me. As I mentioned earlier, my sister is ten years younger than me, and I didn't appreciate her for the first ten years of her life. As I got older, I was able to accept, love and appreciate her, and I now see her as a blessing to our lives.

She would come on every holiday with us, from the age of 12, and helped make a holiday what it should be: relaxing and enjoyable. While I love to sunbathe, my sister likes to be in the sea, so she would play for hours in the sand, building sandcastles with the kids, taking

Feel Good and Watch What Happens

them to buy lunch, to the toilet when they needed to go and she would not say a word about it. She would leave me to sizzle in the sun, and she would take great pleasure in watching my children. They would have fun for hours on end, which made it feel so much better for me. To my sister: you are a diamond. We are indeed blessed to have you in our lives.

I experienced much anger raising my children as both the mum and dad. I had often felt punished; I would beat myself up, questioning what I had done to deserve being alone with two young children.

I did nothing wrong; it was just what it was supposed to be, due to what I was feeling and thinking. My thoughts were the same daily: I was continually spewing the same story, day after day. My conversations were of problems. You might now know why I just wanted to feel good. SO many times, I would say to myself, 'I just want to be happy!!' 'Is that too much to ask for??'

However, life is all about learning. I believe we go through things to get to define our likes and our dislikes, to find out who we are.

Without these experiences, I would not be able to use any of them as an example to help myself and others understand.

I believe it is the way we think, feel, and our perception about who we are and what we are worth that determines how life goes for us. Accepting life so far and forgiving others for the hurt that we may have felt they caused for us, making a decision to take the lead in our lives and feeling blessed for our life experiences thus far and right now, is the way forward. I expected to experience others perception of me, so I experienced what I expected. As I said, the picture painted, my attention and extreme focus on the problem just caused the problems to grow and become more.

We must not allow others to lead us to places we don't want to be, be firm with our decisions, love who we are and know things are always going to work out for us, no matter what.

Anthea Morphitis

Feel Good and Watch What Happens

We need to change our story about our life in the sense of our Self-belief, wellbeing, health and wealth; only then life will start to take a turn for the better. We must accept where we are and surrender to the issues we feel and see ourselves facing each day. Letting go is vital to our growth and happiness. Holding on to negative emotions just holds us in the same place causing ourselves pain.

Anthea Morphitis

Chapter 5: 'In Love'

From about age 17, I always felt the need to be in a relationship. I suppose, due to the fact I didn't have my father in my life, I would search for love via a man. I thought I could feel better about myself if I could feel the love from someone else and often felt alone, so I thought life would be so much better if I were to have a boyfriend. Even though my first two real relationships were disasters, it never put me off; I was very open to meeting someone, and I did.

Shortly after splitting from my daughter's father, I 'fell in love', and vice versa for him (I believe). When I think about it, things moved very quickly, and before I knew it, he was living with us. We didn't give ourselves time to get to know each other; we just jumped right into the deep end. He was single with no children, only 23 and I was 25. I couldn't believe he knew I had children, and he was still interested in me.

The first couple of years of our relationship were fantastic; we would go out to restaurants, bars, long drives and would often travel for short weekend breaks, enjoying one others company. We had lots of fun and laughter together, my children also responded well to him, and I didn't want him to try and take the role of a father figure, he was just my boyfriend.

Unfortunately, as so many of us do, we both expected each other to behave in ways that each of us wanted and when we noticed behaviour that we did not feel helped us towards feeling good, we would blame each other. We both started to focus our attention on the things we didn't like creating arguments, not knowing that we were just mirroring our thoughts of how we felt about ourselves. We were using one another as a way to express our self-insecurities by blaming each other for the way we felt. It is so easy to 'point the finger' and blame the other person for the way we think, and often we feel relief for a split second. If we were to have understood that

Feel Good and Watch What Happens

where our attention goes, energy flows and grows, then we could have consciously chosen to put our focus on the aspects we appreciated about each other, accepting that love is unconditional and starts with self.

I was trying to get someone else to make me happy, and I had put a lot of pressure on him when it was down to me to make myself happy—no one else could do that for me.

Then everything went wrong, way too much attention on the things we did not like and the relationship broke down starting with verbal abuse, and before we knew it, it spiralled out of control.

That's when the relationship took a turn; it was after three and a half years. I woke up one day, and I felt enough was enough; it was not healthy for either of us and most importantly, it was not what I wanted my children to hear, see or learn.

I had to take time out, time out to find myself, to get to know me and have that precious time with my children, giving them my full attention and allowing us to grow as a family without anger. I knew I had to break up the relationship to find myself, regain control of what I wanted and to learn my wellbeing. I had to be happy with who I was, regardless of who was in my life. It was a decision that I thought about for some time, and through will power of wanting a better experience, I just had to find the right time.

Anthea Morphitis

Feel Good and Watch What Happens

The two beautiful souls above are my reasons for wanting to be happy. I know that so many parents are staying in an unhappy relationship because they're scared to be alone. I was one of them. Trust me; we don't have to go through that. We can regain control of our lives, no matter what is happening.

If I were you and you, I would write out what I'm willing to accept, what things are negotiable and what things are non-negotiable to me, my values and make sure I have boundaries in place, communicate to my partner and if onboard. Happy Days!

Still, I am saying we cannot rely on our partners to make us happy. We have to do that part for ourselves.

Tieing in with the above, around November 2008, I had passed by to see a close friend of mine, and on her TV screen, was something that caught my attention titled "The Secret". If you haven't heard of it,

Feel Good and Watch What Happens

The Secret is a documentary and explains the power we hold to create our life, giving many 'real-life' examples and explains the concept of The Law of Attraction and the power of focus, thoughts, words and emotions.

I remember clearly, from the moment I watched it how the 'penny dropped' for me, I had this unusual experience of my life flashing before me, it was like in the movies when the camera shoots back on someone's life. It was crazy but exciting. I just wanted to know everything. I was thinking back and remembering all the new circumstances that had taken place and remembering my reaction, my thoughts, my emotion, and how everything had spiralled. Hooked; I sat with a massive smile on my face loving every second of it, as life began to make so much sense for me.

January 2009, I made a decision that I believed would change my life and ended my relationship, my partner didn't take it lightly and tried for a couple of months to reconcile the relationship, but set on discovering myself alone. I knew if I allowed myself to continue with my partner, I would not do what I wanted to do, and I needed to be alone to teach myself how to let go of the past and rebuild my life.

Find what fills your cup, what you can do for you to feel fulfilled and I'm not saying we have to split with our partners to be happy.

I allowed a lot of pain and hurt, by holding him responsible for the way I was feeling, using the words such as "you should do this or that" quite often, not accepting him for who he was and appreciating him, and also the same from him to me. To be honest, as I said, everything is a mirror to how we are thinking, feeling and our perception. I know you know what I'm talking about, I think 99% of all humans blame others and tell others what they should or shouldn't do.

Anthea Morphitis

Feel Good and Watch What Happens

As I said, we found ourselves focusing on everything that we did not like about the relationship forgetting all the aspects of each other that we fell in loved.

I learnt this does not work; I learnt I am the only person that can make me happy, and others that come into my experience are there to enhance my happiness, not for me to get them to make me happy. That's my job to keep myself happy, not theirs.

Why would I do that to myself?

First and foremost, it was because I didn't know what I know now. I didn't feel worthy; I was facing self-doubt, self-disbelief, insecurity, feeling unloved and mixed emotions about having a man in my life that was not my children's father, and other self-deluded thoughts about me. As I mentioned, everything and everyone is a reflection of us. He was also feeling the same feelings about himself. We both did not have any understanding or knowledge of us as beings. The movie 'The Secret' was the beginning of my awareness of changing the dynamics of my life.

Anthea Morphitis

Chapter 6: The "Secret" Step in the right direction

While working as a PA, I had met my very first entrepreneur, and his lifestyle was just what I always dreamed of having; he was a property developer and the owner of a few businesses. I had, over time, grown to love the idea of becoming a property developer, and had purchased the property that we resided in from the council as my first step in that direction. We became terrific friends, and he inspired me in many ways to start to do what I wanted to do.

Not long before leaving my role as a P.A, we had a conversation, and I had said to him, "If I don't find work here in the UK, I will pack up and move to Cyprus."

I love Cyprus and always hoped that an opportunity would come around for us as a family to reside there. The thought of constant sunshine, swimming pools and beaches ever made me smile. The idea of the children having the freedom to wander the streets, meet with their friends and go to the beach on the weekends while speaking fluent Greek made my juices flow.

I landed a job at the local council and loved the income I received, but disliked the actual position and the fact that my children were attending breakfast and after school club. Working 9-5, with two young children, wasn't what I wanted out of life. It was all too controlling for my liking; I felt like life was "Groundhog Day": every day was the same routine, day in, day out.

I often questioned myself to what we were here for, I had time for nothing but work; my weekends were there to catch up on cleaning and washing. Life was a constant rush, and tedious, I knew there had to be more to life than that! Working in office environments become boring, living like robots! No way! I knew that there was something more; I had just never really explored the endless opportunities.

Feel Good and Watch What Happens

Why? Because I didn't realise that those opportunities were also there for me to take.

Well, all that was about to change. I received a text message while on my lunch break from my entrepreneur friend, asking me to guess where he was!! Well, he was in Cyprus. He stated he would be returning to the UK over that weekend and wanted me to attend a Business presentation that he had recently seen himself and loved.

On the Sunday night of his return, I participated in the introduction, loved it and straight away could see the full potential of this product selling in Cyprus. Three days later, we flown to Cyprus, all expenses paid, with the most fantastic business opportunity. We had dinner with the president of Cyprus is PA and presented the concept and idea to him, his family and his friends, and they loved it. The product had hit the newspapers and had every chance of success.

I was so excited; we sat on the plane, eager with excitement and planning out how everything would work. By this point, I had watched "The Secret", a fair amount of times and had started to become aware of my thoughts and my first encounter of using the Law of Attraction on a conscious level, and it worked.

The question presented to me to move to Cyprus, ecstatic with the idea, the children were at a great age for this to happen: my son was eight, and my daughter was seven, and I knew they would settle very quickly. I made my decision that this would be a great new start for us, especially after gaining an understanding of why things had happened in my past.

As I just mentioned, I had spent a few months before this reading all about the power of positive thoughts and the Law of Attraction, so I was very much like, "Shit, this stuff does work!" All excited, I began to start planning our move abroad.

Anthea Morphitis

Feel Good and Watch What Happens

The excitement was incredible! The kids loved the idea of it; we found a beautiful property and would be supported by the family in Cyprus. It sounds perfect, right?

The build-up was terrific. I would wake up in the morning, eager to start my day. I began to spread the word at work; I spent my working days reading about the best schools for the kids to attend, the best area for us to live in, and looking for a property. The feeling was so amazing. My vision was so real I was beaming all day with excitement. I couldn't stop smiling and felt I was experiencing the power of The Law of Attraction at its best, and Energy was sure moving in the right direction.

I travelled to Cyprus a couple of times for meetings to see how this was going to pan out. I had signed a contract that I would be self-employed, but for the first year and I would be paid a wage, just to have that security. I had booked us one-way tickets, leaving on the 17th of July 2009. I had decided to move at the beginning of the summer holidays so the kids would have time to settle into their new home, area, get to know the locals and for us to relax and settle in.

Anthea Morphitis

Chapter 7: Expecting the Worst

I was so proud of what I had created, and as it got closer to the time, I knew my relationship with my daughter's dad was not very good. We still argued a lot, and there was still a lot of negative energy between us. The time to move was creeping up, and I began to feel fear. I questioned myself, *"Was this going to be this easy?"*

It was almost like I expected it all to go wrong, as that's all I had ever experienced in my life. I still didn't believe things should work out for me. I hit panic, and everything I had learnt went out of the window.

The power of my fear was intense. I was so frightened that my daughter's father would stop us from going; it was starting to eat away at me. No matter how hard I tried, I couldn't stop the feeling of fear that ran through my body.

**'Fear is not real. It is a product of thoughts you create. Do not misunderstand me. The danger is very real. But fear is a choice.'
Will Smith – American Actor, producer and rapper.**

That fear and expectation of everything going wrong happened. My daughter's father, just two days before we were due to leave, had gone to the police claiming that I was 'kidnapping' our daughter. I received a call on my last day at work; it was my daughter.

"Mum, you have come home. The police are here, and they're waiting for you."

I responded, *"Why are the police waiting for me?"*

My mum took the call and explained they wanted to serve me with court papers; she went on to say that I would not be allowed to move to Cyprus with my daughter and if I attempted to leave, an arrest would be the result. (I later found out that if I hadn't touched the court papers, I could have carried on with my plans—so please, if anyone is going through anything like this, before you surrender, use the internet to find out what your rights are.) Devastated by the news, I quietly left the office.

By the time I reached the bottom of the stairs, I was physically sick. I felt like I was going to pass out, white as a ghost, I continued to walk to my car, crying. A police officer had seen the state I was in, helped me to calm down and walked me to my car. I didn't want to tell him what was wrong as I felt he was also a threat to me. My mind was going into overdrive; I felt like everyone was all of a sudden against me.

When I arrived at my mum's, two police officers were waiting there, they asked if we could speak in private, so we headed to the back garden. They explained that if I attempted to leave the country with my daughter, I would be charged with kidnap. My daughter that I carried in my belly for eight months raised loved and cared? Kidnap!!! What the…!!! Really??!!

I had already rented out my property that we had resided in, handed in my notice at work, paid two months' rent for the property in Cyprus and had signed a contract to start work on the 1st September, which was, in my mind, fantastic.

Left faced with a decision: to ignore what the authorities were saying after being served the warrant and carry on with my plans, or accept it and face a court case, which would mean a judge would then decide if it was the right thing for us to do. Not impressed!! In my eyes, I found this to be pure Bullshit!! I felt powerless.

My head and emotions were all over the place. Both my children were upset; no one knew how to deal with this. It was all so surreal; it felt like it was happening, but at the same time, I hoped that it was all just a big joke. I didn't want to accept that after everything I had put into this move, it could be stopped just like that. How could this be? What, I just had to accept this was it? No way!! How could

Feel Good and Watch What Happens

anyone have the right over us just like that? How could this be true? Filled with questions, and when hearing the answers, they made absolutely no sense to me. I phoned my ex, begging for him to drop the accusation, but he just wouldn't. I believe he was on the most significant power trip of his life. He was in full control of this situation, and I think it helped him feel good at the time, in a messed up way.

I felt no choice but to face a court case to permit us to leave the country. I had three options proposed to me, and I felt all three were stupid options, the first was to leave my daughter behind, and she would move in with her dad while I carried on with my move but with only one of my children. Option two was to stay in the UK and face a court case, and the final option was to carry on as if nothing happened and get back to working 9-5 while saving for somewhere to live. What choices!

Advised if I wanted to work, I would be liable for court costs of up to £30,000 and was advised by my solicitor to sign on and stay off work, as this would be a lengthy process and would require much of my time. I was devastated and allowed this to take over my life.

A date was presented to us to be in court to start the ball rolling, attending court was so scary. I felt like I had committed murder, not that I know what that feels like, but you know what I mean.

I remember standing in the waiting area, and a young lady had just had both her children taken off her by the authorities. She was in pieces, crying, screaming in pure pain, while a police officer was restraining her as she screamed, "My babies, my babies, they're my babies! I love them!

Give them back!" My heart sunk. I reached to take her hand, telling her, it would be ok.

I couldn't take it; I couldn't listen and watch. I wanted to beat everyone up, and I wanted to make it stop. Were they going to do this

Anthea Morphitis

Feel Good and Watch What Happens

to me? Was this the power that the authorities held over people? It couldn't be. How can you take a mother's children away? There were so many questions; this wasn't how we were supposed to feel; these were not the experiences I anticipated for us in life. How did it get to this?

The lady's children were not even old enough to understand. I ran outside, sparking up a cigarette to calm my nerves, shaking with uncertainty, crying, questioning why they were doing that to her? I didn't understand. I felt so helpless towards her; I wanted to wave a magic wand and make everything ok for her.

After calming down, I took myself back upstairs and soon called into the courtroom. The presence of my ex standing there was making me uncomfortable, as Solicitors started to present the case to the judge, No one agreed as to what should happen; allegations passed around, the atmosphere was intense, I just wanted out. All I wanted to hear was that I was free to live my life as I pleased, to carry on with my plans, but there was no sign of that happening, just silly accusation.

I wanted to stand and say my piece; however, I was not allowed, I felt like sacking my solicitor and just talking to the judge myself. I knew that wouldn't be a wise move, so I just had to sit back and listen to pure and utter nonsense. As the first court case came to an end, I felt the only thing it had done was to cause more negative emotions for us both.

Well, that was the first of many; every experience at court was like being cut with a sharp knife. It was awful and painful, and every court case filled with high negative emotions, with both of us walking away with more hate and resentment than the last time. Friends and family were so supportive, but when going through something like that, it doesn't

matter how many people support you, you cannot help but feel so empty inside. Between friends, family and I, the court case would

Anthea Morphitis

dominate our conversations. We all hated my ex with a passion. I know hate is a strong word to use; however, that's how we all felt.

I not only faced a court case, but we were living the reality of not living in our own home. Everything I learnt out the window and I had people from every angle questioning my abilities as a mother, meetings with my daughter and her officers. They asked her question after question about me as her mother. I was so angry; I couldn't understand how anyone had the right to question my little girl on the love she had for me as her mother, just because I wanted us to live in my parents' home town. I found that to be mental abuse. Our life put in the hands of the law!! My little angels have always been my 'Why' to continue pushing forward, and below are the smiles of love!

Anthea Morphitis

Feel Good and Watch What Happens

Every day filled with emotions of despair; communicating with a solicitor, driving back and forth to solicitors, discussing and writing statements, going through every living second of how bad it was, focusing day in and day out on all the negative experiences. It drained me; all my energy focused on anger. Rather than enjoying my children, it was all about what he said, she said, etc. I had dropped down to 7 stones in weight and look pretty awful. Every time we had written a statement about one another, the phone calls and text messages would start, filled with abuse. At first, I would react and get myself into such a state. I often felt like I was fighting the whole family as everyone would get involved.

The situation caused feelings of hate, resentment, fear, unworthiness—every negative emotion you can think of, I experienced at the time. My children had become unhappy as they watched and listened to the whole situation. I felt my daughter used as a weapon to control our lives.

It amazed me how the pressure to speak so poorly of each other, from family to friends to the law. It was all about the faults of one another, as a competition for who could find the most flaws. There were lies after lies spewed; all of a sudden, the main focus was becoming what type of mother I was. Consistently put down, being perceived as a Bitch because I wanted to move. I felt like the system sucked, and no one should have to go through that.

We wouldn't have to go through situations like that if we all understood who we are, how energy flows through us and power, we hold as pure positive beings. It's all about loving each other, not hating.

It turned into a case of accused of not wanting my daughter to have a relationship with her dad and her extended family. I felt like a mute—screaming, but no one could hear me!! This court case was supposed to be about us moving and finding solutions for how her

Anthea Morphitis

Feel Good and Watch What Happens

dad and her extended family could still be a part of her everyday life. It just amazed me that it was not allowed to be that straightforward.

I felt helpless. The system was proving to be ridiculous. Was this the best thing for us, just to please one person? Really! I was staying at my mum's, and as you know, my stepdad never resonated with the idea. He made it known to me every second that I was not welcome in his home, putting so much strain on my children and me, and I felt cursed, especially as this was my first time living with my mum, stepdad and sister since giving birth to my son. The relationship between my stepdad and I was one of anger from both sides. I had always felt he hadn't accepted my brother and me since he'd met my mum. I took this in a very negative way, right from the start.

I just wanted to find someone to blame, feeling so down but wanting to feel good. I was blessed with a great opportunity and a life of sun, sand, sea and 100% freedom for my children. Living in Cyprus would have been a dream come true, and I was genuinely proud of my build-up to my move as I had set it all up for myself and my children and felt the universe backed me up with everything in such a natural way. My path seemed very clear; however, I allowed the court case to change my mind from clear to cloudy; I lost sight of what I knew was right for us. I went from knowing to doubting, excitement to sadness and from eagerness to a lifelessness, just because I focused on what didn't feel right to me instead of keeping my focus on what I created. That's how quickly energy moves and how quickly our thoughts manifest in our 'now' reality. Think about it—if I hadn't feared and carried on feeling the way I started to feel, then things would have continued to work out for me, I allowed myself to be defeated. My lack of self-belief creating these situations, and if it t wasn't that the authorities failed, it was my negative attention towards the bodies that shaped what it did. No one was at fault as everyone is attracting to themselves like for like. That's just what I was attracting! It is fantastic when we understand how each person plays a role in our creation as it makes it so easy to forgive as

Anthea Morphitis

we can understand; no one can MAKE us feel anything with their words. We always have the choice to turn the other way and attract what we choose from each person or situation.

"FEAR – FALSE EVIDENCE APPEARING REAL"

I didn't believe that I create my reality at that point. How could that be true? I would not create this for myself, but in the same breath, I knew what I had feared, but I didn't want to admit that to myself. I knew if I took responsibility for my previous thoughts, I would not have dealt with the situation at all. It was easier to blame others. I was no longer interested in the Law of Attraction and questioned everything I had learnt up until that point.

During the time of the court case, the opportunity to move abroad had gone. The company not prepared to send anyone else to Cyprus as my co-workers in Cyprus had only wanted me: even though I had only met them a few times, however they were not prepared to move forward without me. I still wanted to pursue the court case as I wanted to be free to leave the UK and reside in Cyprus.

After reading that, you can see how easily we can fall into that momentum of fear. Could I have avoided most of what we had experienced?? Yes, Yes, Yes, Yes, Yes!!!!

How?

By keeping my focus and attention on my vision, I had put so much focus and attention towards his vision and creation that I had fed it with energy and power allowing the 'situation' to expand. I was forever loading his gun by feeding into the negativity, allowing the bullets to shot my way and hurt me.

Anthea Morphitis

Feel Good and Watch What Happens

Ask, and you shall receive, the universe always has our back. Had I kept faith in the unseen and carried on with my creation, then the opposite would have happened. We would have lived our vision.

We can find anything in our mind's eye to think of that will help us release resistance from what we are feeling, keeping the vision and feeling of what you want present. Which allows the natural rising of your vibration, which then allows what we have asked for to naturally flow to you, as long as you don't doubt. The only thing that is between you and what you want is you!

By focusing on the good feelings like love and appreciating the natural wellbeing flows through your mind, body and soul.

Focus on your beautiful children, the ease of your breathing, the comfort of your body functioning on every level, the sun coming up, the beauty of your natural growth, anything that helps to feel good and last but not least, practices forgiveness.

Doing this allows better feeling thoughts to flow more natural to us, creating positive feelings and favourable circumstances and events.

Letting go of resistance will change feelings of negative to feelings of positive.

Anthea Morphitis

Chapter 8: Mind, Body & Soul

The strain of living in an overcrowded house had become too much for all of us. My stepdad was becoming more stressed and depressed, and it was causing disagreements among the immediate family. The atmosphere in the house was unbearable; the pressure I felt was beyond my belief. I knew I had to move out, but due to the circumstances, I had no idea how I could raise a deposit.

The local council would not house us as we already owned property and advised to take the board to court for them to accommodate us, so I did. I won the court case, and in May 2010, we picked up the keys to our temporary accommodation. I was so pleased; I finally felt like something was going my way. It helped me regain control of my life and begin to feel like me again.

It also helped me prove to myself that I am the creator of my life, and because I kept a very positive attitude about being housed and had no doubt that I would win, we lived what I visioned.

I had, over the past year, rebuilt faith and belief in myself and the Law of Attraction. I felt better about me and found I was starting to receive more of what I wanted rather than the things I didn't want.

Winning the housing case was what I had asked for, and I didn't just ask for it, I knew I would have it, I didn't doubt and had no fear of what I had asked for, allowing the energy to flow. I knew I needed it to keep my sanity, and it felt so good knowing that I had the power to create this. Every time the thought of being in our place was raised, a smile and a positive feeling would be behind it.

Within a week of moving in, I had met a great girl who lived in the room opposite me; we instantly formed a fantastic friendship. She

Feel Good and Watch What Happens

had the most amazing son, with whom I fell in love with, she is a tremendous young lady who, like me, was going through a roller coaster of problems. We were very blessed to have met each other, as we gave each additional strength and would get the best of one another.

She loved the idea of being the creator of our own lives and also embraced it; we learnt so much together. Even though she had her own religious beliefs, she found her balance in understanding and worked with what felt right to her. We became each other's teachers and would bounce off one another. It was so good to have someone crazy like me and had a great personality, and we shared some great times. We would get together every morning and have tea, and breakfast and would pretend that the house we lived in was ours, and spend hours talking about the type of future we would love to live.

The house had 12 bedrooms, and in our eyes, the property had the potential to be the dream home. It was in the perfect location in North London, Enfield and had beautiful surroundings. I was living close by to my friends again and rather than us seeing the reality of the room we lived in; we would avoid saying we lived in a bedsit by creating our version: we would say we lived in a 12 bedroom house, which it was!

My daughter's dad would mock me for where we lived and began a separate court case to get full custody of our daughter, as he allegedly felt that we shouldn't be sharing a room. On our side, we were the happiest we had been in a while. We were free to have friends round whenever we wanted, and I would have my children's friends around as often as they wanted. Unfortunately, the accusations began again, stating that where we lived was not fit for our daughter to live there. He would often try and find every angle

Anthea Morphitis

possible to make life even more complicated, probably because I still expected this from him.

"Life is a reflection of your thoughts and beliefs. we tend to blame others for how we feel, as blaming another feels better in the moment than accepting responsibility, but the truth is there is no one to blame other than self." - Anthea Morphitis

The circumstances were still happening at the time, as I had not cleared out my negative emotions about him, I hadn't practised forgiveness, and my thoughts were still not of love; I had past beliefs that I held and yet to clear out.

My reflection again of my thoughts and feeling of the 'situation' would continue to reflect on me in my life experience until I was ready to want to feel so good that I could think of him in a different light.

Already in the middle of a strong court case and now more questions of my ability as a mother, I believed, at the time, that he thought that eventually I would crash and burn out, but this did the opposite and gave me the ammunition to succeed.

I was again asked every question under the sun and found it very frustrating, as I wanted to be free of it all and just focus on moving forward. The desire to move abroad was dead; however, I kept having my focus clouded by things that I knew would only hold me back. This time, I took a different approach when questions were flying my way, I had answers that felt good to me, as I approached the situation with as much love as I could find within me under those circumstances, and I knew we were starting to head in the right direction. I did find it was unfair on my children as we didn't care where we lived—we were just happy to be together and do what we wanted again. I did everything in my power to not dwell on accusations and kept myself feeling good. I would always tell myself that everything was okay and things could only get better, with my thoughts being more positive and my overall feeling being good life was looking better.

In late November, I had asked my mum if she could have my children stay with her for a couple of weeks while I took time out for me. It was time for me to clear my head of every event and person that felt so negative to me. I wanted to restart my life again; I had picked up so many unworthy beliefs about myself; I wanted to find a way of starting fresh. I spent day and night searching on YouTube and Google and reading books on how to clear negative emotions about myself and others. I locked off from the world for a bit, knowing that would be my best way of moving forward and finding peace in myself.

One of the first processes I came across was meditation, and I thought it sounded ridiculous; however, I didn't care, so I tried it. At first, I found it a nightmare trying to quiet my mind; however, I was determined to quiet my mind and realised I needed patience, I had to focus on my breathing, redirecting focus and thought. Within a week of doing this every day for at least 15 minutes, I did it! It was a very blissful experience that I became hooked. I had read that I had energy blocks and for me to move forward, I would have to unblock them, for when energy channels are blocked, manifesting is very difficult because our minds are not focused on what we want. The act of manifestation it is focused upon all the unwanted things.

Refer to Chapter 14 for a full description of Meditation.

I have learnt some powerful practices; the next I'm sharing is taught by Abraham Hicks's and is 'The Book of Positive Aspects'.

Where this process aims to write positive aspects—what is good about a person, place or situation that you already believe—it is

Feel Good and Watch What Happens

about looking for the already- present good in a person, place or situation in your life.

Write at the top of a page a subject, and I started with the name of my daughter's father, under his name, I wrote things I can quickly appreciate about him; for example, "He is a great salesman." I believed that, so it felt good to write that and I carried my list on from there. The next subject could be my body, my home, etc.

The next step was to write every topic that came to mind, even if it was a subject that could potentially upset me like an ex-partner that, and spend just 10 minutes a day writing something positive or something you can appreciate.

What this process does is redirect thoughts, training our minds to focus on good things, making it easier to think positively automatically. Raising our vibration, realising resistance and allowing ourselves to attract the positive aspects from each person situation, etc., as we are focusing on good feeling thoughts, reflecting in our everyday lives.

This daily process has changed each one of my relationships for the better. I listened to endless numbers of ways of clearing out negativity and acted on them. I tried NLP (Neuro-Linguistic Programming) and Tapping, which helps us to free ourselves from negative feelings and beliefs. I found this to be very helpful, and I wrote pages of things I would like to experience; I created vision boards and spent hours listening to inspirational and self-empowering material.

Focusing on happy memories as I could think of, taking my attention away from my negative thoughts and feelings of my ex and his family to as many positive aspects of them as possible.

Anthea Morphitis

Feel Good and Watch What Happens

In all honesty, I found it difficult at first, however, within a few days of writing positive aspects of myself, others, and the beauty of the planet, my mind opened to better thoughts of him and his family.

I was feeling better about myself after feeling like everyone was looking at me as a massive failure and felt undervalued as a person due to the things I had been through and had allowed others' opinions to control how I felt. However, by writing lists of positive aspects, within a short space of time, my efforts were beginning to show up in my everyday life.

I wanted to be able to forgive everyone; holding baggage of un-forgiveness tears us apart, and I knew it. I learnt something recently that I didn't realise at the time, which is that un-forgiveness is simply a judgement/perception of someone and that by not forgiving, we are only hurting ourselves as it is we who must walk with those feelings inside us. We only stop our own lives from moving forward, not theirs. Let it go; forgive everyone and everything. Don't let history hold you back as I had.

"Opinions ain't facts, take them and let them go" - Rapper, *Chipmunk*

Anthea Morphitis

Chapter 9: Court Cases

Through May to November, I went through very mixed emotions. There were points where I had felt like there was no way out, questioning, "What is the point? Why?" I owed people money, my friendships were breaking down, nothing seemed to be going my way, and I had felt low. Taking that time out was needed and helped me to clear my mind and soul out of many thoughts and negative emotions. The process of meditation and positive aspects only takes 10- 20 minutes of our day and is so worth it.

I had cleared so much out of my subconscious mind, replacing my negative thoughts with positive thoughts of love. I was feeling like a new person. Every part of me was starting to feel alive again. I become happier and happier, which was reflecting on my children, and they were also becoming more satisfied by the day. I could see that life is a reflection of the thoughts I thought about myself and others.

After clearing my head, I decided to focus on raising the money to move and get us into a three-bedroom house, just like I knew we deserved to have. With the help of friends and family, I had raised the money. I choose to move to Chelmsford, where my daughter's godmother resides, from the time I had children I had always stated that didn't want my children to attend secondary school in London, I tried to move a little further out, so the next best place for us was Chelmsford. My daughter's Godmother was kind enough to give me a job in their family business and offered me pretty good wages. I knew I could keep up with the rent and appreciated the support I received from her and her family; they pulled out every stop for us.

Together we visited the local schools, and both children accepted into our chosen school. We were so excited; we found the perfect home with three bedrooms and a park leading off our back garden.

Feel Good and Watch What Happens

I paid a deposit set to move, school just walking distance from the property. Their friends were also so excited about having my children attended the same school as them. I have a very close relationship with my daughter's godmother and often drive back and forth to Chelmsford. I love the feeling of open space and believe we would have enjoyed living there.

I have always felt that my daughter's godmother is an angel sent from heaven; she is a fantastic person and has been a rock to me in my life.

After getting everything ready, I proposed the move to my daughter's father. I was very confident that it would be ok, especially as I had spent many hours writing positive aspects about him.

Guess what he did—he opened yet another court case, objecting to our move. Yes, another court case had started within the two existing, this was a joke, right? I felt like I was on a merry-go-round that was never going to stop so I could jump off.

No way can he object; it's a 25-minute drive away! This time, I didn't think this would happen, by the time a date had set, I had lost my deposit, as the court date was after our move-in date. The property was very quickly snapped up by another family. I attended court and granted the right to move without a second thought by the judge; however, I still felt like I was back to square one.

The reason I feel the situation reoccurred is due to the reality of other court cases still in motion. I didn't realise my focus and attention on them was creating more. Life is trial and error. Also, forgiveness, meditation and positive aspects are something that needs to be practised often.

Daily if possible as we have blockages that take time to clear, and even when we think we have done enough and something unwanted manifests, it just means we have more forgiving to do.

Anthea Morphitis

Feel Good and Watch What Happens

My ex would try every angle possible to make life hard for us. I believe the reason why he found it so easy to do this was because of the advice he received from the solicitor, and the law states that as he is the father, it is legally right for him to do this.

The judge was livid! She was not impressed with the fact that he had objected our move, especially as so much up raw was made about us living in one room. Tears came to the judge's eyes, she ordered a five-minute break, as she needed a minute or two. I could feel her disappointment in my ex, and she looked me straight in my eyes with such sadness and walked out. I felt like strangling him, I wanted to shake him, and tell him to stop. He had also not turned up on a few court dates on purpose, to help drag the other court case as long as possible, as he knew it would be adjourned without his presence.

This particular judge had been my judge through all the instances, so she had gotten to know my personality. As the case came to an end, she had warned him that if he tried to take me to court again for anything else, she would personally have him arrested for wasting the court's time. She had seen what I had gone through and sympathised with me. I had presented all evidence of my move, and the judge could not make sense of why he would object; hence, the decision to permit us made without a second thought behind it. I knew I had very little income. I couldn't even think of any ways to raise the money again.

We'd put so much work and emotion into yet another move; the children were excited still only and then let down again. I felt powerless.

Remember, The feeling of powerless will only attract more to feel powerless about through people, circumstances and events.

This time, I was in a better feeling space along with better thoughts when my ex stopped us moving to Chelmsford. At a guess, 50% of my thoughts were positive; therefore, I had dealt with the situation

Anthea Morphitis

Feel Good and Watch What Happens

pretty well. I freaked out for a bit; however, my frustration didn't last long. To be fair, by this point, I had been through so much that I kind of didn't care. It was what it was. It happened this was him; I couldn't change that about him. I had a choice—my choice was to either focus on him or focused on what I wanted. I had to accept that I had no control over his words or action and that I only had control over myself and my perception.

Following that particular case, the other court case to move abroad was still in motion, and a three-day trial set for April 2011 in Oxford. All our previous cases held in North London; Oxford is roughly an hour and a half drive away. It was going to be a different judge to the one we knew. I had reached the point where I felt it was all too much; the judge set for my final case knew nothing about me, my children or my ex. How could he possibly decide on our life just by reading a few statements made by others? We had a Jury, which I thought was crazy.

I'd had enough. I wanted it all to end. I pulled the plug on the trial—it was wrecking everyone's lives. The courts had requested witness statements from friends and families, and they were going to have to be cross-examined in court and would have to travel to Oxford for three days. I didn't feel like that was fair to do that to the people I loved.

Anyone would have thought that I had committed a lifetime sentence crime. Unprepared to drag my friends and family down anymore. I wish someone had sat with me at the start of this and explained the trauma this would cause. I didn't want anyone to experience going to court and have them take three days out of their family and working life for me; it was just too much for me to ask from others, this wasn't a game, and I certainly was not having fun.

I surrendered with my head held high. I believed the best thing to do was to just to walk away, rather than trying to control my thoughts and emotions on this whole situation. A final court case set for

Anthea Morphitis

Feel Good and Watch What Happens

December 2010, where only my ex and I had to attend, with my original Judge, also advised that once my daughter becomes 12 years old, I would be free to go anywhere in the world without having to attend court.

I also wasn't prepared to move my children abroad at the tender ages of 11 and 12. My daughter only had a year left of junior school, and my son had already started secondary; there was no way I would do that to them. When this had started, they were both attending junior school, so the timing had been perfect. I knew things had to change; I couldn't live my life like that anymore. I wanted so much more for my children and me; I knew life was not supposed to be like that. I knew, deep down, we were supposed to be happy. We had experienced way too much. I was down to just seven stone, fading away, and my children had experienced stuff that I never thought they would.

On December 22nd, the night before the final court case, I was anxious; however, I was determined to keep positive, hearing the words 'You're free to go' in my mind. I did everything I could to stay happy. I had a restless sleep but got up nice and early, ready to do this. Before I knew it, my palms were sweating with anticipation of what was going to happen. I kept a good vibe on my way to court, singing away in the car, trying to stay as fresh as possible. I arrived, patiently waiting to hear our names.

Morphitis vs That's me. Ok Deep breaths, Anthea, it's ok. I

carried on repeating to myself that it was all going to be ok.

"All rise." The judge walks in—silence—you could hear a pin drop. "You may sit." As we sat in silence, awaiting the verdict, my mind was going crazy. I kept on repeating the words I wanted to hear:

Anthea Morphitis

Feel Good and Watch What Happens

"You're free to go; you're free to go." Then I heard them: "Miss Morphitis, you are granted full custody of your daughter and are free to reside anywhere in the UK."

A sigh of relief, do I cry? Do I laugh? What do I do? The court case was over!! I felt like it was all pointless, but at the same time, it felt like it was worth it such mixed emotion. I smiled and thanked the judge. As I walked away, I felt the feeling of freedom. I stood outside the court, looking up at the sky. Is this the end? It felt so surreal: two years of living a life of 'uncertainty', feeling like I was not able to move forward in my life, being questioned on my every move. Wow, this is the end.

Wooooohooooooo!

I sat in my car, making phone call after phone call, so happy that it was over, It was all so overwhelming. After a few calls, I drove home, full music blast and a big smile on my face, realising I could choose any path I wanted. What a good feeling, knowing I could finally move forward. I had taken control of my thoughts and feelings, and things had worked out for me. Living with fear is one of the worst things we can do to ourselves; the quicker we learn to let go of doubt, the faster we can take control and move forward.

As it stands today, in 2013, my daughter's father has moved away for the next six months to deal with his issues, and he sees our daughter once every 3-4 weeks. She still visits her Nan and extended family every other weekend but has no real relationship with her dad; his relationship with his mother and sisters has completely broken down.

When I first heard he was away, I have to hold my hand up and say I had felt a slight bit of hurt and anger, as even after all this time.

I had questions I wanted answers, no one prepared to talk about why he would be away for so long.

Anthea Morphitis

Feel Good and Watch What Happens

During the court case, accused of taking class A drugs by my ex, accused of being mentally unstable, of being an alcoholic—you name it, I was accused of it!

I often say if someone is accusing you, it means it's something they're doing, I didn't have proof maybe I'm right perhaps not, all I know is his not around for the next six months.

The truth will always show up in the end. The Law of Attraction is something we just can't get away from—what we give out; we will get back. I allowed myself to feel what I was feeling but very quickly brought myself back to where I stood in that present moment. I take full responsibility for the way I was feeling. I would not change the experience for anything, and I now thank my ex for the journey we went on, for giving me a fantastic daughter, and this has been part of my journey to finding my purpose in life.

It's incredible, as I realised I still had that little bit of despair deep down, but I am now over it!! I know better than to be that person. I am having the best time of my life right now, and I feel way too good for anything like that, and love knowing that I was totally in control of what I wanted to happen and I have made my choice.

Like I have always said, and I stand by it: it is my daughter's family, and I appreciate them being in our lives. I hope that her dad can come away from the place he is at in his mind, realise how good life is supposed to be and appreciate what and who he is and the abundance he has in his life. I hope he becomes the best he can be, and also feels good about the experiences he is experiencing on his journey.

Single parents: try not to let this be part of your reality. There is no need to fight anyone, but there is always a need to take control of you.

Focus on what you want to create; you have the power to feel good and control your thoughts, words and actions. Become aware of the words you speak and the emotions you feel behind the words.

Anthea Morphitis

Feel Good and Watch What Happens

Many people's attention was on my 'situation', and as many do, they have an opinion on what you should or shouldn't do. In these experiences, I couldn't stand on my head in enough different ways to satisfy everyone's desires.

"Care about what other people think of you, and you will always be their prisoner" – Lao Tzu

Anthea Morphitis

Chapter 10: Two Steps Forward, One Step Back

Early one morning, after dropping my children off at school in March 2011, there was a knock on the door. To my surprise, we had to leave the hostel. As the court case had now come to an end, I was no longer eligible to be housed by the council. It was up to me to stand on my own two feet now, which was fair enough.

You might already guess I had already had the thought and question of 'what would happen with my place once the court case was over'?. I felt a little fear that we would be asked to leave, and that's what happened. Do you see how powerful thoughts are? So many people don't realise this and think that everything is happening to them, when in fact you are doing it to yourself.
I had a few days to sort myself out and get out; however, I still had the question of what was I going to do again. I felt I had no choice but to move back to my mum's. I even, at this point, did not believe I could afford a place of my own as the court case had only finished in late December. I had managed to find myself work; however, I had only been working for a couple of weeks when I found out we had to leave the hostel, and the work I had taken on was commission based only, so no sales equalled no money. I had not earned enough to afford a place of my own yet. My mind closed to solutions, and the only logical thought that came to mind was to move in with my mum. When I tried to think of getting us a property to live in, my doubtful thoughts took over in a split second, questioning myself on the 'how's'.

"The How's are the domain of the universe. It always knows the quickest, fastest, most harmonious way between you and your dream" – Rhonda Bryne, The Secret

Anthea Morphitis

Feel Good and Watch What Happens

We moved back to mum's, and I felt like a failure again. I lost all self-esteem. I was sharing a bed with my daughter; our friends were not allowed round as my stepdad wouldn't allow any visitors. We were living in Hertfordshire; I didn't have a car which was massive for me as I bought my first car when I was 17 and have always had one. I felt like we were in the middle of nowhere. I was a grown woman; this had to stop.

It was time to believe again in my ability to feel good about myself; I had done it once before and knew I could do it again. I was feeling and focusing on all that I thought I didn't have, feeling down about myself, feeling the lack.

I wanted to know how to become happy, regardless of what was so in my face of reality. I wanted to know how to use my mind to look past what was there in front of me. I was determined, feeling stripped of who I was, and I didn't want ever to experience anything like that again. I knew what I wanted, and that was to enjoy every second of life. I wanted my children to grow up with great memories; I wanted everyone to get on and live a 'normal life'—one of love, not hate, ease, not a hardship. I started reading and exploring all aspects of how I could benefit from being aware of the Law of Attraction and continued to practice appreciation and forgiveness.

I began to practise meditation again, focusing on what I wanted, thinking and feeling the outcomes I wanted to experience, and I slowly guided my mind to better feeling thoughts.

It was time to align myself with my desires; as much as I was learning, I still was at the teething stages of my understanding, putting my practice into my everyday life. I had read and listened to enough about the Law of Attraction that I had a good enough knowledge of taking the conscious journey to change my beliefs to what I knew did not do my children and me any justice. I had held us in bondage with my thoughts and feelings, and I wanted that to change. I knew I could change my beliefs by practising new thoughts

Anthea Morphitis

daily to ones that would create good feeling experiences in so many different pleasing ways.

Determination is one of the keys to a successful outcome: when we are determined to do something, we will see it through without given up as our determination will drive us to our destination.

So much that has happened that I will not involve, as I am at peace with lot's of past experiences and have accepted them for what they are. I also don't believe it is fair for me to express things about others, as it was also their personal experiences, and they have had to go through their journeys. What my experiences were with them is not who they are, just what I was attracting from them with my perception/judgement of them.

I have always had great friends around me, ever tried to make the best out of anything and everything. I have always had a great relationship with my children and my sister; they gave and still do give me the strength every time to get up and try again. It never mattered how much I went through; I would always eventually find the determination to get up and try again, and I appreciate myself for that.

"No matter how you feel, get up, dress up, show up and never give up" - Regina Brett, 45 lessons The plain Dealer

As I had spent day after day working on my beliefs, emotions and mindset, opportunities were starting to show up. Like a ray of light, life was becoming exciting again.

An ex-colleague of mine that I had worked with at the local council had called me after two years of no contact between us, a very bubbly and positive character that I had connected with and understood the LOA. When I received her call, she was full of excitement, and her energy instantly rubbed off on me as she spoke to me about business opportunities she was involved. She was so excited that we had connected again. She shared this business

Feel Good and Watch What Happens

opportunity, inviting me to watch a presentation about this business—no questions asked, we immediately arranged to meet to head off to The Hilton Hotel in Central London to attend the presentation. As I walked into the room and looked around, everyone had smiles on their faces, filled with positive energy, and the room felt so light, free and welcoming. I met a whole new set of people, people with aspirations, people that were running their businesses—entrepreneurs, property developers; everyone just so inspired me. My new-found energy and positive outlook to life grabbed many people's attention, and a few people that I met were so interested in finding out more about me. What a feeling! It proved to me what feeling good about me could do for my general wellbeing and state of mind. I felt, for the first time, that I had left the old me behind and found a whole new Anthea.

The presentation was a Network marketing opportunity; it was my first encounter since my break in Cyprus, a way to build my own business from home and based on the internet, learning ways to receive residual income. I was on a high; it was so exciting. As the speaker began the presentation, he also spoke a lot about self-development. I was amazed, and everything I had been learning had just been presented to me by someone else, like a reflection of my thoughts coming straight back at me. "So, there are others that think like I now think? Wow!" It was at that moment that I realised I wanted to teach self-development and the Law of Attraction. I was so excited about the information he was projecting and my understanding of what he was saying that I just wanted to interact. I wanted everyone to know how excited I was. At the end of the presentation, I sat with the presenter and had a fantastic inspirational conversation, which was the start of our new friendship—a friendship that inspires me and has taught me so much. He travels the world teaching self-development, and I am so proud of his achievements in life and aspire to walk in the same direction.

Anthea Morphitis

Feel Good and Watch What Happens

From that day forward, I met so many great people; network marketing opportunities were coming to me left right and centre, and the universe was delivering to me lots of excellent feeling opportunities and people. I was attending presentations in central London at least once a week; each person that I interacted with was on the same page as me, reflecting my good feeling thoughts and emotions. Every person I met was such an inspiration, many entrepreneurs, so many people with a purpose to life: that's what I wanted—a good outlook on life. The more focus and attention I was putting towards everything, the better life became.

There were four people in particular that I met, all a few years younger than me, and we instantly all connected. They were all on their journey to success; they were such an inspiration to me, so much passion for learning, endless ideas and a ray of light. We spent so much time together and grew a fantastic bond and connection. We were all pretty new to Network Marketing and embraced the journey together.

Even though all these significant circumstances presented to me, I still held a negative feeling every time I walked into my mum's home. I would dread going back, expecting the worst every time. For some reason, I found it very difficult to hold a reasonable good feeling from my stepdad. I could hear him in my head, putting me down. He believed I should have a 9-to-5 job and that Network Marketing and thinking positive was just a dream that would never be my reality, he perceived life as crap and money can't flow unless you work hard at a job that doesn't serve you. He certainly had no belief in me succeeding at anything, and this was just a reflection of my thoughts and expectations of him towards me that I had to learn how to change. I struggled mentally with feeling right about him; hence, my stay at my mum's was short-lived. As much as I tried, I just couldn't seem to master how to clear my negative thoughts and emotions of my stepdad, and I just expected the worst from him.

Anthea Morphitis

Feel Good and Watch What Happens

I also want to highlight that he is a good granddad to my children, and I appreciate his support with my children through everything I have attracted to myself. As I said, these are my personal experiences; we invaded his space. I understand why he couldn't handle us being in his home; after all, there were three of us. I have also learnt so much from him. I love and appreciate him for who he is, and I know that he is proud of me. I have said some hurtful things to him to in the past, and I hope he can forgive me for the way I have reacted to some circumstances.

Anthea Morphitis

Chapter 11 Becoming Homeless & The Turning point

On my arrival home one evening in November 2011, my stepdad decided he no longer wanted me to stay due to an argument that had taken place a couple of days previously. He had packed my stuff into suitcases. The problem we both had was we were not afraid to say what we wanted, and we can both be very Bull in a China Shop-ish if you get what I mean. We sat and spoke about what he was feeling, and he wanted his space. By the time the conversation had come to an end, it was 1 a.m. I stayed another night and left in the morning,

I was devastated, and so were my children. I finally felt like I was in the right place, then this! How much more of this could I take? Is there someone testing me? My good friend that lived in the bedsit next door to where I previously lived kindly offered I stay with her, but as it was a bedsit, there was nowhere to sleep but on the floor.

I had again feared this would happen but hoped that with enough attention on other things that it wouldn't happen. However, subconsciously, the fear was there, and I would sometimes get visions of my stepdad asking me to leave. I tried to fight the thoughts and images; however, I have more recently learnt and practised that fighting the mind does not work. We must get to the core of the issue within ourselves, face it and forgive ourselves and the other before we can clear it out of our minds and be free of it.

From my first night there, I was no longer able to perceive the house as the 12 bedroom house that I used to see it as although I appreciated the roof over my head and the kindness of my friend, it felt like a prison. I do understand and not just understand I overstand how people get themselves to the point where they want to take their own lives. I was there myself; however, I have been fortunate enough to have people that love and care for me in my life and the

Feel Good and Watch What Happens

determination to want to understand why we face circumstances in our lives. Still, I also know that many people don't have anyone to turn. Hence why I feel books like mine can help people keep faith that things will work out as long as your prepared to be selfish enough to only care about how you feel in each living moment with a determination to live the life you know you deserve.

After moving, my world began to crumble again; I felt embarrassed to attend any events; everyone seemed to have money in their pockets—something I struggled with—their own homes, and so on. I was not allowed in my mother's house as my stepdad didn't want me there—also because of the way I was feeling about myself.

I found it very difficult to deal with; all I wanted was to wake up to my children. I just wanted to give up.

I had spent Christmas day alone as my stepdad wouldn't let me stay at home and spend Christmas day with my children. I didn't want my children to come to where I was staying as it didn't feel right for my babies to see me like that. My children were missing me like crazy; that was the most challenging day of my life, not being with my children on Christmas day.

On their return to school, they started too really misbehave, and things were spiralling out of control. The feeling of my reality was way too hurtful to be able to see past what I was living. I had lost my mojo. I find it fascinating how our surroundings dominate our thoughts and feelings, The reason why it happened in the first place was because of what I was thinking and feeling, which then lead to manifesting those thoughts into my reality.

Shortly after New Year's, I got myself into a state. I had a breakdown.

I stood in the local park, crying uncontrollably, being physically sick. I couldn't breathe; not prepared to live another day without my children. Something had to change!

Anthea Morphitis

Feel Good and Watch What Happens

I didn't seem to be able to overcome my thoughts and had spent way too much time and energy dwelling on the Negative, which led my ideas very quickly to thinking of ways to take my life and who would look after my children if I was no longer living in this world. At that moment, I felt like the biggest failure in this universe. People were walking past, asking if I was okay I was just shouting "Leave me alone!", *"Please just leave me alone!" "I want to die!" "Please, I want to die!"*

At that moment, my friend had phoned me, he had phoned about three times, and I just kept ignoring his calls. I finally answered, and he heard the state I was in *"What's wrong?" "Anthea; what's wrong?"*

"I can't do this anymore; please I can't do this anymore," I said. *"I want my children back. I just want to die!"*

"Anthea; calm down, I can't help you unless you calm down." My friend knew what had been happening; however, I had never expressed my hurt; I would just make out as if everything was ok. He continued to talk to me; the sound of his voice was so calm and soothing. It was like his spirit was there with me; he calmed me down with his words and the tone he spoke them in. He reminded me of who I am—a mother of two beautiful children who love me, a creator, a high spirited being with high aspirations, and he reminded me of the power that I held within me to turn what was happening around. I believe the universe sent him to me for that moment. I think he would have been the only person on the planet who could have calmed me down at that moment the way he did.

I had slowly calmed myself down, still not being in control of my breathing; however, I was slowly starting to feel better. My friend stayed on the phone to me until he felt confident enough that I would not bring any harm to myself and asked me if there was anyone I could call to come and get me. I thought of my good friend that I had met when I was only three months pregnant with my son while

Feel Good and Watch What Happens

working for a bank and we have been friends ever since. I felt she was the right person to call; I promised him I would call my friend and call him back to let him know I would be safe. I called her; the second she heard my pain, she dropped whatever she was doing to come and pick me up. She was there within 20 minutes. She kindly offered to let me stay with her for a week or so while I got myself together mentally and emotionally, and I appreciated her support. We got back to hers, she made me a cup of tea, and we sat up until the early hours of the morning talking. For her, this was a shock as she knew me to be so energetic, happy and bubbly. I think I'd had enough of being mentally strong, and everyone would always say, *"Don't worry, you're strong. I know you will get through this."* Sometimes we don't want to hear that; we just want to crawl into a hole and come out when everything is ok again.

Between the advice given to me from friends and my determination to make things right again; I gathered my thoughts again, made an action plan and took the step to regain control of my life and get my children back under the same roof as me.

Minute after minute, hour after hour, I would envision myself taking my children to school. I would talk to them on the phone every night and put my spirit there with them, experiencing the moment like I was there with them. We would Facetime each other so I could see them and say goodnight to each other while being able to see them. I love technology!!! I would act out all the things I wanted to be doing, consciously creating.

I soon rented a room from a girl that I had met at Networking Event and began to envision what I wanted to happen next in my life and took control of my thoughts. I had my own space to think and create. It was on a high as my friend, and I had developed an excellent relationship, which made it a whole lot easier.

Anthea Morphitis

Feel Good and Watch What Happens

She embraced me living there and would invite me out with all her friends on the weekend. I was again meeting so many new and good people, and life was on the up.

I hired a car to pick up my children from my mum's in the morning, driving them to and from school. Our daily conversations consisted of the things we would be doing once we moved into our new home. We got specific and discussed numerous aspects of the house, such as decorations, room layout, the parties we could have and so much more! Doing this allowed me to put forward the idea of my family living together again.

I would pre-act out in my mind what direction I wanted to go and what I wanted to experience next in my life. I began to perceive life as if I were the director of my movie and could create how I wanted my life to be. I still found myself in situations, but the difference was that I had a better understanding of why I was experiencing these circumstances as I became aware of my thought process.

"When you trust in the laws of the universe, prepare yourself to receive all that you have asked for. Take your focus off the problem, and appreciate all that you can see and trust me it will be!"

Now, living in a three-bedroom house with my children, I feel proud, I learnt so much, and without going through any of these experiences, I probably wouldn't have the same inspiration to tell my story and how I did it. I certainly wouldn't be the person I am today, had my life played out differently; it would not have been my life!

Anthea Morphitis

Chapter 12: The Law of Attraction

The Law of attraction - Simply put, that in which is likened to itself is drawn. So, for example, if I am thinking I hate someone or something, then my emotions are going to be similar to drawing to myself like for like. The universe will deliver to me more of the same to match my thoughts and feelings via people, circumstances and events to match, It is worth perception and thinking positive rather than negative as we are sure to receive the reality we are thinking.

My understanding of who we are and the Law of Attraction has been through endless hours of listening and watching Abraham Hicks's, watching videos on YouTube, reading books like 'Think and Grow Rich' by Napoleon Hill and 'Ask, and it is Given' by Abraham Hicks. Also having lots of conversations with others and last but not least, my experiences and implementing and practising what I'm learning. I now know all my lessons are a blessing to me as part of my path/journey to writing this book and teaching personal development. Whether myself or others perceive these experiences to be positive or negative, I feel blessed to have experienced them.

I found that the more I spoke, the more I understood—and the more I understood, the more it was being projected through me through my words and actions. I realised how and why people are experiencing what they are experiencing and was feeling extremely gifted. I am now able to help others make sense of what they are experiencing and why. I truly appreciate the level that I am at, at this point.

"Appreciate and enjoy the beauty of the world. Focus on the good and attract more of the good into your life right now. Be happy and appreciative for all you have in life, and more good will come." Anthea Morphitis

When you use your imagination and project good feeling thoughts, the universe responds to that. As the law states, you get back what you give out; you will get more of what you are feeling and thinking

Anthea Morphitis

now. I now love and appreciate who I am, everyone that has been and is part of my journey and the power of alignment, vibration and thoughts.

> *"You cannot have an unhappy journey to a happy ending" - Abraham Hicks*

The best way to understand the Law of Attraction is first to know that we live in a vibrational Universe, where everything is energy.

Whether we are speaking about humans, cars, money or houses, it is all energy, consisting of atoms, electrons, protons and neutrons—both positive and negative.

Our brain transmits a frequency, just like a radio station tuned in. For example, if you're tuning your dial to 100FM, you cannot hear what is being broadcasted on 107FM, as these are two different frequencies. While optimising your dial from 100FM to 107FM, you will experience an infrequency that will let you know that you are not tuned in. By focusing on one frequency, you can hear what broadcasting. We work in the same way: our brains transmit and receive energy, and we transfer that energy at different vibrational frequencies, with as much or as little power and focus as we choose.

As our brains transmit these frequencies, this affects physical matter. As everything is made of atoms on the planet and all atoms are made of electrons and protons, which are made up of vibrations, everything on this planet, including us humans, consist of the same thing—ENERGY!!

An example of this is when you think of someone, and then receive a call from the very person you just thought of, that is your brain transmitting a frequency and received by the other person. The frequencies come into alignment as you have both tuned in to the same radio station (each other) and one gets the urge to pick up the phone and call the other.

Anthea Morphitis

Feel Good and Watch What Happens

Most people would say, *"That's weird; I was just thinking about you!"* The reason for the connection is because the frequency was pure; there was no doubt, just a genuine thought of each other, which caused the impact to act and then to connect.

I often experience this; just today, I got the impulse to call a good friend that I have not spoken to in a while. As soon as I called her, the first thing she said was, *"OMG, I've been thinking about you!"*

As time goes on, I have become more and more connected. More often than not, I think about something, and it happens!!

When I think thoughts of something I don't yet believe, and I have doubted my thoughts—for example, *"I am buying myself an island today!"*—I know it.s possible to buy an island. However, I don't believe I can purchase an island today. Which can lead on to doubtful thoughts, causing an infrequency and misalignment,

A path will not open and become visible until you believe and align. I will not just yet experience the manifestation of buying an island until my thought of this becomes pure, and I believe in the reality of it becoming real. Once in belief, I will watch the universe open a path to make this become my reality and then I will be purchasing an island!!

Once we trust, believe and realise what we have thought of, things will play out, one after the other, at the right place, right time and when we are feeling at your best.

By focusing on an idea and believing in our concept, more feel-good thoughts of the like will continue to come to mind; we get the momentum rolling. By replacing thoughts of doubt with feelings of joy and appreciating all that I can, what we want will happen!

The Law of Attraction says vibrations attract similar vibrations: or like attracts like, similar to what goes up must come down (Law of Gravity).

Anthea Morphitis

Feel Good and Watch What Happens

If we're feeling happy, we will attract happy thoughts and circumstances into our experience. If we're feeling bad, we will attract unhappy thoughts and situations into our life. That's why, when things appear not to be going our way and we put our attention there and feel the feeling of feeling bad, sad, or hurt; we attract more circumstances and events to bring feelings of alike through the frequency that we are vibrating. The same principle goes for when we are feeling good; we attract more good feeling circumstances and events into our experience.

What we think and feel is what we experience in our physical experience. We cannot feel wrong about something and have it turn out good; it is two different vibrational frequencies, and it goes against the laws of the universe. The key is to feel good, no matter what is happening in our lives—not using our surrounding or others to determine how we think.

We live in a vibrational Universe, and every single thing that is vibrating is putting out to the universe a magnetic pull, which is drawing everything to us, wanted or unwanted. We have a unique ability to use our minds and feelings to transmit a vibration, and we have the choice of what our thoughts are and where we choose to focus our attention, in terms of what we attract to us.

If you can imagine yourself standing in the middle of an empty field as giant magnets and everything you are thinking at that point is being drawn to us, wanted or unwanted.

We close our eyes and just visualise that what we are thinking is smacking straight into our physical bodies and feel it, whether it's a car, house, food, debt, lover whatever the thoughts. By visualising what we want and feeling the feeling of having it with intension and belief, it must become.

Anthea Morphitis

Feel Good and Watch What Happens

"We are transmitting frequencies 24 hours a day seven days a week, and the universe is responding to every thought and feeling"

The thought is the reason for vibration, emotion is the response to the vibration, and the mind is to guide from an emotional desire. We have a feeling response to everything when we think we respond with our feeling, so what we are feeling is our indicator of what is in our vibrational content. It's a point of attraction; everything we offer is on a vibrational level, which then brings our manifestation to what we are thinking and feeling and the universe is not hearing our words; it is always responding to our vibration. When we speak, we vibrate; therefore, our vibration can never lie. We cannot trick our vibration into pretending to be happy.

Wherever we put our attention, the laws of attraction state that it must expand, therefore, more attention to the very thought, the more we hold it as our truth.

"A belief is only a thought you keep thinking" - Abraham Hicks

I find this quote by Abraham Hicks to be very powerful, especially when we grasp and understand the power of our thoughts and feelings.

"You are today where your thoughts have brought you; you will be tomorrow where your thoughts take you" - James Allen

As we think, thoughts actualise and materialise around us and eventually become part of our experiences through focus and attention to those thoughts wanted or unwanted.

By truly believing in the object of desire and focusing onto it with pure intention and belief, this will lead to that object or goal realized on the material plane. The universe provides a path to deliver what we focus on; besides, negative thinking will manifest negative results.

Anthea Morphitis

Feel Good and Watch What Happens

"The action of the Mind plants that nucleus which, if allowed to grow undisturbed, will eventually attract to itself all the conditions necessary for its manifestation in outward visible form." -
Thomas Troward

Anthea Morphitis

Chapter 13: The Power of Now

Understanding the power of now: whether you are thinking about past, present or future, you are doing it now. Every thought we think is creating now; it actualises around us, so it is always good to be aware of what we are thinking and feeling at all times as this gives us the power of now and helps us to stay present.

We will always get what we want if we believe we can have it; thinking of the ifs, buts and maybes will hold us back from receiving what we have asked for, the universe cannot deliver what we do not expect.

If we do not expect to receive it, then how can it be? It again defines the laws of the universe. Everything you have ever asked for in your life is waiting for you to realise so you can experience; we just have to be happy with our now and allow the abundance to flow; align ourselves with our desires. The way I believe in doing this, which has worked for me, is to feel positive feelings, reach for positive thoughts, speak and act in accordance to what you want and feel what it feels like to experience it. We don't necessarily have to only focus on that particular desire for it to manifest; we just have to feel as good as we can in each awakened moment. I have found a great attitude to have is: "I am where I am, and it's ok!"

I used to have the view: "If I could just have what I have asked for, then I would feel better", not realising that I had to feel good NOW before I can recognise the experience!!

We seem to spend so much time thinking of tomorrow, that we seem to forget a compelling truth and that is we are living in the present!

"Now is what you got all the time, there is never tomorrow, tomorrow is an illusion; it will be eaten up by today, now is all you got" - Abraham Hicks

Anthea Morphitis

Feel Good and Watch What Happens

All our power is within us here and now; what we are thinking and feeling now is what counts. Many plans for tomorrow and worrying about things not yet happened, Whether we imagine a positive or negative outcome, we are in control the overall result. By being aware of what we are thinking, we have the power to influence.

For example, we may have found ourselves saying things like, "Oh, I knew that would happen", not realising the reason why we knew it because we felt it and thought it, therefore, it manifested into a life form.

By the power of focus at that moment and the attention to the situation, the outcome becomes what we expected, and maybe you have found yourself blaming someone else for your creation.

An example: while I was going through the court cases, I had been blaming my ex for everything that I was attracting to myself, at the end of each court case we would use abusive language towards each other and feel like absolute crap. We would often fight and disliked each other, blaming one another for the way we were feeling. I did not realise I was the one in control of what I was feeling. I felt like absolute crap and was getting what I was putting out there.

I would now say to anyone: if you're going through anything with the father/mother of your child/children, take a step back and think about what you are doing to yourself, children and others around you. I just believe it's not worth it.

It doesn't matter what they have done in the past, by focusing on what

you believe to be wrong; you are just going to carry on extracting those aspects of them and continue living what you do not want. If you keep talking about it and feeling down, you hold yourself in a place of despair and apart from what you ultimately want.

Anthea Morphitis

Feel Good and Watch What Happens

Gain control of what is rightfully yours, by controlling your emotions and reaction to situations. Hold a clear positive vision in y our mind of the outcome and feel it like it has already happened. You can do this by saying 'Thank you' for everything working out for me, regardless of what reality is showing you. Remember: reality is just the result of our previous thoughts and feelings; it doesn't mean we have to live the same thing day in day out continually. We have the power to change situations, here and now.

Through continuously working with my thoughts and feelings, I have proved to myself that the better I feel about me, and the more I find things to appreciate, the better life becomes.

Life is precious, and we are worth so much more than living a life of fear, arguments, etc. We only live this life as the personality known as us once, so we owe to ourselves and the people we love to take control no matter what we feel another has done to us. Don't worry about what they're doing; just focus on what you want. Remember: by not forgiving, you are holding yourself back, and carrying unwanted emotions.

I now believe Life is here to enjoy, not to fight others over things I want, but to know I have asked for it; therefore, I will receive. However, that only started to happen once I was happy with myself and practised forgiveness,

There is a massive world out there, more than enough resources to back up what we want. There may be lots of things that we have yet to experience or places we may not even know exist, so many good experiences that we could be focusing on and then experiencing. We really can choose what we think and how we want to feel. It is down to you what happens in your life. We can start from any point and begin to reach for better feeling thoughts, and once we start, it becomes so much fun.

Anthea Morphitis

Feel Good and Watch What Happens

No one knows better than you; no court/judge should have to decide for you. I experienced first-hand what it feels like to spend so much time, and energy in that situation and I would love if others could use my experiences to avoid that despair, and hope to find a way not to take that deep dark road and see the light before it gets out of control. Find a solution without having to go through the madness of court, communicate calmly.

By taking my attention away from the things that bothered me about my daughter's father, forgiving him for the hurt I was feeling and refocusing my attention what I found to be positive, the court case was able to come to an end. We were all able to move forward, rather than keeping us all in bondage. We were able to feel freedom and love for the first time in a long time.

I can proudly say that we have a great relationship now as I no longer blame him or anyone for the way I am feeling at any point. I now appreciate those experiences as they led me to learn about myself and understand so much about who I am and to believe in myself. I trust that whatever I want has to be. I no longer doubt; I just know that things will work out and if I was to open my door right this second, and everything that I had and have ever asked for was to land on top of me, it would be too much. I wouldn't be able to deal with it.

I now expect most days that I will experience different experiences and know that every second is the manifestation of how I'm feeling. Don't get me wrong: I still have to work on those negative self-sabotaging thoughts, especially when it comes to money.

I am working on my expectations of receiving a natural flow of money. I sometimes find that the demands of having two teenage children can be overwhelming, not from them but in general in everyday life, and one of the worst feelings is feeling like you don't have enough money to buy general stuff for your children.

Anthea Morphitis

Feel Good and Watch What Happens

However, I am determined to work in this particular area and know I will be in vibrational alignment before I know it. The money will continue to flow to me, more comfortable. I spend time visualizing and remind myself of what I already have in motion. I have a huge advantage that I didn't before: I now know how to focus on abundance, meditate, write lists of positive aspects and forgive past situations to do with money.

NOW NOW NOW is very powerful. Now is what is creating every second of our experience. When you think about it, you may realise, every second that passes by becomes the past, but in each second that it becomes the past, we are thinking thoughts now. Those thoughts are creating and becoming future experiences. Whatever we are feeling now is actualising around us now!

Now that is worth thinking about, right!?? It's exciting when we grasp that. Well, it was for me anyway, and still excites me now.

Often when I am in deep thought, and I imagine the fact that my thoughts are actualizing around me, I get so excited. It's a cool thing to get one's head around and so much fun!

So we are where we are; we can't make everything become what we want it to be right now, but we can feel good about now and care about the future, slowly accept what has happened in the past, and find something, anything that can make you feel good as often as possible. I know sometimes it just seems like an impossible mission, but trust me, it can happen; believe in the power you hold within. Believe you me; I know how it is to struggle with understanding in my wellbeing. You would think that it would come so naturally to us; however, I think it depends on what type of experiences you have experienced as to how easily you can forgive and move forward.

As I mentioned earlier, there are always two sides to any situation. We can look at the negative, which doesn't feel great or the positive, either way; it will send a signal to your brains, which will then be

Anthea Morphitis

followed by vibrationally matched thoughts. Your choice which end of the stick you put your attention on.

For example: If you would like to go away on holiday, look at your bank account and realise you have little money and a small income right now. Three children, we're going to feel not too good probably, however, if you can say to yourself 'It is what it is and I am open to the possibility of more money coming to me', then you have opened a doorway to allow the money to come to you.

"Believe. Act as if. Live like you already have it" – Unknown

Think about this: if you create your reality, and you have a choice, and your choices are to worry and think thoughts like, 'I don't want to feel stuck at home with no money, children and no holiday' or thoughts and conversations of 'How nice would it be to go away with the kids for two weeks. Imagine the fun you would have' get on the internet and spend time looking at the places you would like to go and imagine yourself there with your children and make it real. Imagination with a belief is compelling, and you can do this regardless of what your bank account is showing you at that moment. We are the directors of our lives. As I mentioned, it's like directing a movie: you direct your thoughts and have the choice to choose what you think, and that is one of the beauties of us as human beings.

Don't let situations control you, take your power back, be playful about everything; make it fun to play around with your thoughts.

The universe will bring circumstances, people, and events to make it be. When you know what you want, it must be. By deliberately being conscious, visualizing, feeling and specific about your desire, you're letting the universe orchestrate the 'how's', let go and trust!

A path will become visible; you will realise that even if we don't recognise the first clue, we will identify the second and if not the latter, you will identify the third. What I am saying is that it doesn't matter if we miss the first boat. Don't worry; there will always be

Feel Good and Watch What Happens

another. In other words, a way will consistently be shown to us until we recognise it, and when you do, you will be booking your holiday.

Every year, I knew without a doubt Alex, Sophia and I will be going on holiday, even though there were times where I didn't have two pennies to scratch together, and I would have to search down the sides of the sofas, hoping to find some money to buy milk and bread, but I didn't care. I just knew I would be going away.

Every year, I would call my family in Cyprus and tell them to expect us. I had no doubt we would be heading to Cyprus, the same date every year. My son had his first holiday when he was just ten months old, and my daughter when she was a year old.

I held an expectation and felt we deserved a holiday. As I said, I didn't care what bills I had, as I knew they got paid; I would ignore my bank account and focus on the fun of being in Cyprus. By speaking about it before I could physically see my flight tickets, experiencing it in my mind, having others expecting to see us, then it had to become and every year it did.

"You can either focus on Poverty or Wealth sickness or Health; the choice is yours"

I cannot highlight enough how important it is to feel satisfied and happy with yourself. When you look around and think of the people in your life, and find things you can appreciate, practising writing them or even just have those thoughts of appreciation in your mind, what happens is because you are focused on the good, you will naturally feel good. The good feelings will continue to roll, experiencing and receiving daily more people, things, circumstances and events to appreciate.

A little appreciation exercises to try: which I did and still do now and have found it to be robust and helps me feel good.

Anthea Morphitis

Feel Good and Watch What Happens

Wake up a little earlier every day, spend just 5-10 minutes in the morning writing a list of all the things you appreciate, either about yourself, others, nature, material things whatever you choose as long as it brings a smile to your face. I believe this exercise starts your day off in a good positive feeling which heightens your vibration and leads to your day being full of good feeling experiences.

First of all, this helped me to have an excellent start to my day, and second of all, as days passed by, I started to notice the difference. I found from the very first time I did this; things began to change for me. I was receiving more things to appreciate daily. My list becomes longer; I found it easier to think of something to enjoy, as more was being blessed to me daily to be appreciative for.

I could make decisions and knew what I wanted to experience in my life, building a new thinking system.

I always appreciate when I awaken in the morning, and I can breathe without even having to think of breathing. I think that is great. We just expect to breathe right, but I believe these are things that we should appreciate, the parts of our body that we take for granted. I never appreciated the fact I can walk, talk, breathe, move, see

and hear until I met others that couldn't, and added these things to my list.

Laughter is great; I love it when I laugh so much that I feel like I just finished doing 100 sit-ups and my cheekbones hurt from it. That is such a better feeling than feeling angry, right?

I was humming away yesterday and felt my vibration, it became a powerful moment for me, as I placed my hand on my chest and listened to the sound I was emanating and explored how we vibrate our energy. It brought me to a new level of understanding than I had the minute before I started humming. Try it and feel what you get from it.

Anthea Morphitis

Chapter 14: How We Feel is The Indicator to the experiences ahead

To live can mean living a life of suffering, as many are unaware of the power of their emotions and mind, and we appear to live in a world that is not perfect to the eye. Due to constant negative media, whether through TV advertising, news or schools, everywhere is promoting negativity. When it is only as perfect as we perceive it to be, many choose only to see the imperfection and ignore the wellbeing.

We strive for a better life; however, many are not able to keep their vision of what they would like to live. During our lives, it is inevitable that we will experience suffering such as sickness, pain, tiredness, old age, and eventually we pass. We can also experience psychological suffering such as frustration, disappointment, fear and depression.

There are many different things we can go through psychologically, but there is also the other side, the positive side, of life's experiences, which we perceive to be the opposite of the above. We have different degrees of positive experiences such as abundance, appreciation, freedom, ease, prosperity, love and happiness and seeing life to be imperfect and incomplete, living an eternal journey.

> *"Poverty is not an accident. Like slavery and apartheid, it is man-made and can be removed by the actions of human beings" –*
> *Nelson Mandela*

Could you imagine if the news was full of good news, news that inspired people all over the world, full of inspiring stories of love, wealth, wellbeing, abundance, prosperity?

Lots more people would wake up with positive energy and conscious of their thinking patterns, with a sub-conscious full of positive

Feel Good and Watch What Happens

examples rather than the current news that fills people with fear and anxiety.

Everyone will inevitably pass away one day. As happy moments pass us by, left with only memories, we tend to wish our lives away instead of savouring every precious moment that we live, appreciating life and seeing growth to be a pure blessing.

Transient is the origin of suffering, it is our attachment and ignorance to the temporary things, this is not just the physical things/objects that surround us but also ideas, and in a greater sense, all objects to our perception.

The ignorance of the lack of understanding of how our mind is attached to impermanent things is why we put ourselves through suffering. With our desire, our pursuit of wealth, passion, craving popularity, all the outer elements of who we are, as the objects of our attachment are transient. Their loss is inevitable; this is why suffering will generally follow because we crave it, and when not receiving, we put ourselves through the pain of bad feelings and self-deluded thoughts, creating beliefs of unworthiness.

An object of attachment is also the way we see perceiving "self", the idea of what we understand 'self' to be. 'Self' is a delusion, as there is no abiding self. Everything is energy; what we call 'self' is just an imagined entity. We are part of this expanding universe and are forever expanding beings. We can choose to suffer from self-thought or prosper with self-thoughts.

Although this is a gradual process, slowly but surely you will be able to take control of the thoughts you think, guiding your mind to think thoughts that are in alignment with who you are.

> *"You have to find a way of thinking the thought that gives you relief, before the things around you can change. Thought and vibration are one of the same; a practised thought is a practised vibration, which equals a point of attraction." - Abraham Hicks*

Anthea Morphitis

Feel Good and Watch What Happens

Maybe we're at a point in your life where we feel like the world is against you (I can assure you it's not). That may be hard to hear right now. Still, with a desire to want to feel good and live a fulfilling life, you will slowly be able to turn that around by taking your attention off the situation and redirecting your attention to something that is working out for you.

For example; if there is someone in your life that you feel brings you down and dominating your thoughts, then take your attention away from them and, focus on the people who bring joy to you by writing as much positive stuff about them as possible.

In time the person will either reflect the positive aspects of what you have focused on or no longer be part of your life, and please don't let that scare you. The same stands for a situation you feel are dominating your thoughts; something will change as you are no longer in vibrational alignment with the person or situation.

Re-directing the energy can no longer expand on the negative; it must now expand on the positive due to our change of attention. By continually reaching for better feeling thoughts in time, you will be in control of how you think and feel about anything. This exercise is compelling; It works like a dream, and I love it.

As I mentioned, Forgiveness is also a significant way to gain control of self. It allows you to be free of your past, leaving the past to rest and ready to create the best!. We're expanding beings; we don't stand still, and the earth is spinning in every moment. We have to learn, let go of negative emotions and thoughts, to create a better future.

"Forgiveness liberates the soul. It removes fear. That is why it is Such a Powerful Weapon" - Nelson Mandela

Communication is also vital so If something is on your mind, then express it, find a solution, move on and let it go. Remind Yourself that things will always work out for you.

Anthea Morphitis

Feel Good and Watch What Happens

When you accept your natural wellbeing, you can trust that whatever the issue is you will find the answer. If instead, you choose to dwell in the problems day in day out then indeed be prepared to continue to live the issue.

Vibrating a negative emotion will reproduce the same sentiment that we don't want. Let go and move on.

Is the problem a problem or your perception of it being a problem? How you want to perceive it, your perception and my perception do not necessarily have to be the same, for something to be right or wrong. What I choose to regard as the right does not mean I'm right, it is just my perception; hence, why I now do not believe in arguing as my opinion is that it is not right to be angry with someone just because they have a different perception to me. Different viewpoints do not mean I'm right, and you are wrong; it is just a perception.

As women, we want to call friends or ask as many people as we can for their opinion, and ask that question, "What do you think I should do"?

Just remember the more focus you put towards the problem, the more the problem will expand in and spread to other situation in your life, creating issues that can potentially be dragging on for days, weeks or even months. The universe will always deliver to you like for like via different circumstances, people and events. Then we wonder why this keeps on happening!

I recently moved into a new home, which has been fantastic; however, after only a week of moving in, I had a run-in with the neighbours. One evening, the couple who live next door to me knocked on my door, aggressively —I thought someone was breaking down my door. I opened the door, and to my surprise, the couple both looked angry. Confused, I asked politely. Are you okay? Before I could finish my sentence, the lady started ranting and raving about the noise coming from my house. (Remember, we have been

Anthea Morphitis

Feel Good and Watch What Happens

here for one week, so we are still unpacking boxes, and my understanding is, the landlord had lived here alone for five years, so no one heard a sound from here) This lady was so angry; she was foaming at the mouth, not something I had ever seen before! She explained with anger, "I can hear you going up, and down the stairs, I can hear you moving the beds" and went into details of the things you would expect to hear from anyone has just moved into a new property. I calmly apologised and said I would do everything I can to move furniture quietly. I knew from that moment, living here could be a problem. I have two teenagers who like to have friends around, play Playstation and listen to music!

To cut a long story short, at first, I allowed these neighbours to change the way I felt and started telling others what had happened, speaking very negatively of them. The more I said the story, the more the couple turned up at my door or thought it was a good idea to bang my walls.

I decided to stop feeding into the negative energy by not sharing telling every time they created a problem and instead appreciated the fact that I have neighbours, and most importantly, that everyone is different and that they don't know what I know!

The experience makes me smile and appreciate the fact that I can love, regardless of how others behave.

We really can just forgive and let go; create new perspectives, and wake up every day, treating it as a new day. It is your choice!

As I mentioned, I practise at least 15 minutes a day of sitting in a room learning the technique to meditating (which results in a still mind, allowing the mind to go from negative to positive). I would just sit, being aware of my present moment, focusing on the sound of my breathing, simply forgetting everything that bothered me.

Anthea Morphitis

Feel Good and Watch What Happens

Meditation is an increasingly popular technique being used all across the world for various reasons that are unique and individual to each human being who does so.

The definition of the word meditation is any form or family of practices in which practitioners train their minds or self-induce a mode of consciousness to realise some benefit. Simply put, those who meditate know that the answers to all their questions and problems are found within themselves and nowhere else.

It does not just stop there. The results of meditation are vital to optimising our health; we must have a complete balance of the mind, body and soul. With new technological advancements, there are many meditation practices which only require 15 – 30 minutes of relaxation time per day which you can practise anywhere.

The initial mission statement for anybody who mediates is to teach our busy minds to become quiet, to release our psyches from the stress, anxiety or depression that can be from our physical reality. All those who meditate to bring peace and serenity into their lives using their preferred technique will rapidly benefit from a deep feeling of being at one with their inner selves, beginning the process of healing and improving their mental and physical health. Regardless of the reason for practising it, new and ancient meditation techniques alike will set in motion the most important journey and discovery of life. When first starting meditation, we may still find your thoughts are very dominating, and might feel like your thoughts are in control; however, through practice, you can put your mind at peace.

"Beginner's breathing meditation."

Sit comfortably and close your eyes. Take a few moments to "simply be". Notice whatever experienced at the moment—sounds, physical sensations, thoughts, feelings—without trying to do anything about it. Continue like this a little while, allowing yourself to settle down.

Anthea Morphitis

Feel Good and Watch What Happens

Now bring your attention to the breath. Simply notice the breath as it moves in and out as the body inhales and exhales. Notice how the breath moves in and out automatically, effortlessly. Don't try to manipulate it in any way.

The mind will wander away from the breath—that's fine; it doesn't matter. That's a part of the meditation! When you notice that you are no longer observing the breath, bring your attention back to it. For each intake of breath make it last 4 seconds, holding for a further 4 seconds, and then exhaling for 4 seconds out of the nose.

Let all of your experiences—thoughts, emotions, bodily sensations— come and go in the background of your awareness of the breath. Notice how all your experiences—thoughts, feelings, physical sensations, awareness of sounds and smells—come automatically and effortlessly like the breath.

After a few minutes of 4-second inhalation, holding and exhalation, start to go deeper, inhale through the nose for 7 seconds, hold the breath for a further 7 seconds and finally exhale for 7 seconds, this time out through the mouth. After a few more minutes, return to comfortable, relaxed breathing that suits you.

After about 10-15 minutes of focused breathing, the incessant stream of thoughts should have quite mellowed out. If you are doing this meditation without music, bring your attention beyond any sounds you may hear and focus on the deep silence and the empty, spacious void of darkness. Within the dark, visualise a pure white light. Go further into the light, bathe in it, feel the stream of positivity and warmth firing in your chest/heart area, your soul light; visit this space as much as you can for fulfilled healing.

This meditation will bring oxygen, nutrition and energy to the cells, heart, lungs and digestive system. Strengthening these supports the health of all of the other parts of the body and can assist the body with healing (mental or physical). Merely putting your attention on

Anthea Morphitis

your body brings energy to it. You can use this meditation to enjoy a sense of wellbeing and enliven your body.

In time, you can become aware of the tendencies of your mind. You will see how it resists specific experiences and tries to hold on to others. The natural settling down of the mind allows you to notice these underlying tendencies and creates the possibility to let them go.

As the saying goes "Practice makes perfect". Do you agree?

Many may say, 'I don't have time', create the time! If you can find time to eat, talk, work and sleep, then we can find time to relax and meditate. We will see that a lot more solutions to things will come to mind. It's worth trying, right?

Many are so used to doing the same things and tend to forget there is a whole world out there surrounded by pleasing nature and beautiful scenery. Even going to the local park feels like a breath of fresh air. We can change how we think in seconds; when we see the trees, flowers, hear the birds sing, watch the squirrels chase each other. Who cares what the government is doing, when you have nature to focus on, the kids love it, and we can enjoy it too.

I also find watching comedies is a great way to get me feeling good; my personal favourite is Lee Evans; I literally stop breathing from laughter. There are so many great movies that are at our fingertips. I say thank goodness for the internet, even our mobiles—we have access 24/7 to lots of things and people who can help us to feel good. It is just up to us if we choose to use that to our advantage or not.

If you haven't guessed already, my point is to FEEL GOOD!!! I wouldn't say it if I had not personally done it myself. It has changed my life in so many ways; every relationship around me has improved on every level, just because I forgave and found endless ways of feeling good.

Anthea Morphitis

Feel Good and Watch What Happens

You might well be in a place where life is where you want it to be. Then, in that case, carry on doing what you are doing. If you're on the other side, then this has worked for me and may very well work for you too.

You will find your children want to be around you more and you want to spend more time with them. Our thoughts change, new ideas come to mind, and overall life becomes fulfilling.

Anthea Morphitis

Chapter 15: Setting a New Point of Attraction

Meditation will most definitely set a new point of attraction and is a great way to start your day. We are born pure positive beings, and through contrasting experiences, we find ourselves focusing on the problem, causing us to feel negative emotions. However, how long we allow ourselves to feel those negative emotions determines how life goes for us. The underlying reason to why we feel negative emotion is because we detach ourselves from who we are (pure positive energy). We pull ourselves apart from our natural wellbeing and allow our attention to be focused on negative situations way longer than needed, causing our bodies to react due to the stress/pressure we feel.

It sure serves us better when we become solution orientated, taking situations with a pinch of salt, knowing that a solution will occur. As long as we are open to solutions and not focused on the problem, then we can allow the wellbeing to flow through us.

Well, it is time to set a new point of Attracting by following and practising meditation and appreciating from the second you awake. First thing in the morning, Appreciating your beds, covers, pillows, the fact that you had a good night sleep or whatever it is for you. Appreciating is also a great way to break out from the beliefs our parents and others have taught us. We often take on parents' beliefs while growing up, which may not serve you today.

Creating new beliefs takes time; this won't be something that will happen overnight, and for some, it might seem like this is farfetched, but you have attracted this book into your life. Everything I have spoken about is my experiences of what I was thinking and feeling about myself and others manifesting in my life. If I have been able

Feel Good and Watch What Happens

to retake control of my feeling and thoughts after a lifetime of anger and negative thinking and feeling, believe me, anyone can.

Take time to understand your overall thoughts, ask yourself often what will be the result of I continue to think this way?

I find by keeping that image of a giant magnet in my mind; it helps me remember that I am continually attracting to myself. I imagine my thoughts as objects smacking and sticking to me and question if the ideas are something I'm happy to experience.

Experts have expressed, we have, on average, 70,000 thoughts a day, so we obviously can't control all of them, but we can be picky about the ones we want to think about most.

We are all offering a vibrational signal now, not later or tomorrow—it's now. Our frequency sets a pattern of attraction, allowing rendezvous with people that are of interest to us and vice versa, stimulating conversation or not; doors opening or not, returning home in the evening feeling satisfied or not.

The thought is the reason for vibration; emotion is responding to vibration, ideas guided from an emotional desire. Think about it: we have a feeling response to every single thought that we recall. So as we think, we respond with our feelings, and our belief is the indicator of our vibrational point of attraction.

Everything that we offer is on a vibrational level and will manifest, and life is one prominent manifestation of how we are feeling.

As we become conscious about what we are attracting and how we feel, our vibrational frequency rises to a higher level, and the more the goodness of what we want can flow into our lives. We can receive what we have asked for, as quickly or as slowly as we choose. We need to be clear about what we want, state it, own it and know it. By holding a thought for as little as 17 seconds, the Law of Attraction brings another thought of alike. By the time we reach 68 seconds, we

Anthea Morphitis

Feel Good and Watch What Happens

have now got the energy into pure motion. Our thoughts begin to form around us, and manifestations become visible in physical or word form and realise how the subject at hand surround us.

I find this extremely fascinating and love the idea of this, just knowing that as I am thinking my thoughts, they are forming and becoming part of my experience. The knowledge alone gives me faith and belief, helping me in my everyday life.

Have you ever had the experience of buying a new car, all of a sudden, everywhere you go you seem to see this car? Law of Attraction in action! I have fun with this, and while out driving, I will think of a particular vehicle I would like to see and notice how quickly they appear. It's great fun.

I also do things like visualize parking spaces, so when I go into town, I like to park in the multi-storey car park and have a particular area that I like to park because it is right next to the lift and the ticket machine. I always get the space that I want because I get the picture in my mind of me parking my car. I feel it, see it and then play out the scene in my mind, so when I arrive, I am then able to experience what I imagined in my mind's eye, and it's great. To be honest, this is how I now live my life.

It is so important to feel good, but we can't pretend to feel good as vibration cannot lie.

I had mentioned earlier that as I was growing up, I would always have a smile on my face, but inside I was hurting. I thought that because I would smile, everything would be ok, but nothing seemed to get better. That's because my vibrations cannot lie. What I am transmitting is the truth; no matter how much I tried to hide it with a smile, I was continually getting back what I was feeling from deep within.

Learning to get rid of those excuses that kept me feeling miserable, and replace them with reasons to why things should work out for me.

Anthea Morphitis

Feel Good and Watch What Happens

I began to create a new story a story of wellbeing, abundance, love and prosperity. I found something that I liked and spoke about it, and I talked to people that made me laugh and had pleasant conversations with, and boy, it felt good.

In the past, when I would visit my mum's, the talk would be very detrimental. It seemed to always be about people who died in other countries, what someone said, what happened in the war, how many people lost their lives, what body parts hurt, how many tablets they both take. My mum's favourite word used to be terrible! My mum is also trying to become acutely aware of her thoughts, and thus far is doing pretty well.

Before the conversations were enough to make me want to scream, I also used hold the energy of my mum being unwell because of the words she constantly spewed and with what I could see with my physical eyes, I knew what she was doing to herself. The terms used in the household were negative. However, I brought myself to learn to accept my mum and her way of thinking; she is old school. I used to use so much energy trying to explain what she was doing to herself until I gave up and accepted her for who she is.

My mum thinks it is excellent that I have found a new way of thinking and is very proud of how I have turned my life around through changing my perspective on me and life. She is now starting to believe that life can change and get better.

I will continue doing what I am doing, knowing my mum's and everybody's wellbeing, and I think in time that with me as an example to wellness and prosperity, she will get what I express. Until then, I will carry on sending my good positive vibes her way and seeing her as I know her natural wellbeing to be. I now refuse to hear or see illness within my mum; I only see her wellness, and in time she will see it too.

Anthea Morphitis

Feel Good and Watch What Happens

So we keep laughing, smiling, loving and appreciating, as all these are positive feelings creating positive thoughts and raising our vibration, causing a change in our point of attraction.

I find that when the contrast of life gets to me, and I know that the feeling of anger is right on the brink of breaking out, I allow myself to feel that, as it is what it is. However, I then I stop and think, take deep breaths and do anything I can to help me reach for better feeling emotion.

One thing that I find works for me is going for a drive. I currently reside in Hertfordshire, which is very green and full of beautiful views. I drive for as long as it takes. I put music on and sing my little heart out (even though I could break windows with my voice). I don't care; I bop away, appreciate my car, my surroundings, my radio, the artist that I am listening to— whatever I can do to change and take control of my emotions.

It has considered me some time to be this conscious, but I have stuck with it. I cared more about how I felt more than anything that surrounded me in my life, especially as I was left standing with nothing at one point and had no choice but just to appreciate me and the power I knew I hold within.

I bring myself into focus and think of my children laughing. I hear their little laughs in my head. Even when I'm living something I don't want, I hold my focus of positive feeling thoughts for as long as I can, by appreciating anything. I enter my mind into that playful place of creation and have fun with images and conversation that I experience there and then—not physically, but I know it will become part of my real experience and I just have pure fun with my thoughts.

I was setting a new point of attraction when it comes to debt.

Let's say your reality has it that we are in debt, that debt is causing you to feel fear, uncertainty and confusion, so your focus is on the debt. What you are doing by focusing on the debt is creating more

Anthea Morphitis

and other circumstances that give you the same feeling of what you're allowing the obligation to make you feel. Things could feel as though they are spiralling out of control. The more attention you put towards these circumstances, the more the energy flows towards that which is causing expansion.

You might find you're speaking to friends and family, with deep emotion of fear. Rather than doing that, you could talk to the citizen's advice bureau and set up payment plans, that might be helpful and help you feel better about the current situation knowing there are solutions. You could then write out what you want and be specific about it.

Once you are focused on solutions, and you are specific about your outcome, ideas can come to mind. And may find yourself experiencing those nice 'A-HA!' moments, thinking, "Wow, I spent all that time worrying, and all I had to do was that!!" and now you are changing your point of attraction.

"Worrying is like sitting in a rocking chair. It gives you something to do, but it doesn't get you anywhere" – *Unknown*

I remember my friend calling me and saying, "Right. Enough is enough. Let's sit down and work out what you owe, work out how much you can offer, and start making calls and showing a willingness to do something about the debt." I was so surprised to find how supportive every single creditor was. For a long time, I thought the problem would disappear if I simply didn't think about it, but we have a conscience, and my subconscious mind was always aware that there was a problem. So, that feeling would come to the surface and cause more anxiety again, until I took control and worked out how much I needed to bring in to be able to clear off my debts. I also had loads of debt that had been caused by others, which had initiated that feeling and thoughts of, 'Why should I pay?' feelings, anger and resentment. However, I accepted it for what it was and got on with it.

Anthea Morphitis

Feel Good and Watch What Happens

While making the calls, I could feel myself becoming lighter. My shoulders became relaxed, and the tension was easing; I was able to see the light at the end of the tunnel. A couple of weeks later, I was employed and bringing in more than enough to cover the arrangements that I had put in place. I am now financially stable and creating a better and better present and future for myself and my children every day, and I am building an empire for us.

Expect things to work out for you and keep the faith. One thing I have learnt and have become so aware of is that it was only my thoughts that stopped things from going my way—fearing that something wouldn't happen for me—what an illusion that was—stumping the natural wellbeing flowing my way. Now, when something doesn't work out how I thought it would, I expect something even better to come my way as I believe in living a good life.

"I find that the more willing I am to be grateful for the small things in life, the bigger stuff just seems to show up from unexpected sources, and I am continually looking forward to each day with all the surprises that keep coming my way!" - Louise L. Hay

Here is an exciting and useful example of the Law of Attraction: I am just on my way home from meeting friends for dinner, and the topic at the table was predominantly about men/relationships. Right now, I'm on the train, in front of me is a reflection of the conversation we were just having, two young guys; the talk is about girls and the reaction of a certain female when one of the lads tried it on with her—a similar conversation to ours. It's amazing how the Law of Attraction gives you evidence of your focus and attention.

I now attract great people into my life. I have met some fantastic people. Here's a quick story: I was driving around Hackney with a few of my business partners—who I must say are all fantastic, ambitious, great people. We were in a back street—lost. My friend

Anthea Morphitis

Feel Good and Watch What Happens

had spotted a car parked up on one of the side roads with the lights on. My instinct was to turn the car around and beep my horn. The vehicle had blacked-out windows, and my friends in my car were shouting to carry on driving as they were frightened. Well, I didn't listen, I pulled up and wound my window down, so did the car next to me. To my surprise, it was a very famous UK rap artist!! He was so helpful and down to earth—a lovely experience, my friends were screaming with joy! Only you Anthea, only you, this would never happen to anyone else! We laughed and joked about it, and everyone was on such a high! I have met many well-known people, and I believe this is due to my expectation, high vibes and the way I think!

I had partnered up with a college, creating business events. The last event we held together, my college had invited a business trainer to speak about the business he works with, which is raising people's profiles in specified areas of work. Well, blow me down!

What a blessing he turned out to be for me. He had invited everyone who had attended the event for a free one-to-one session to find out each individual's directions. I am now on a course which helps me define my ideas, working closely with a mentor. I took the opportunity with both hands, feeling the inspiration to act. I had asked the universe for help, and guidance with an idea I had to and the universe delivered. I had no idea of what presentation would be about, but the universe had brought us together for the benefit of what I had asked. All this has come around through me trusting, believing and being happy with where I stand. Life is unfolding the way I expected, but better!

"Change what you think and feel about yourself and others, and notice how the reflection of your thoughts and feelings will be attracted straight back to you." Anthea Morphitis

Anthea Morphitis

Chapter 16: Limiting Beliefs

As only a small population understands the Law of Attraction, it seems that many need to see manifestations before they can believe they can have what it is they have asked. Exactly how I used to be. "Ask, and you shall receive" is the motto. By taking control of your feelings and thoughts, you can also begin to change your limiting beliefs about yourself.

What is a limiting belief?

A limiting belief is when you want something and do not believe you can have it, by mentally putting a limit on the things you can have through your personal feelings about yourself. I proved to myself that if you are not aware, your Surrounding can play a big part in what you believe you can and cannot have.

We pick up many of our limiting beliefs about ourselves along our journey through all the experiences we have experienced, which then holds us back from what we desire. Many will make up excuses for why they can't have what they have asked for when really, the excuses are just excuses. Nothing more and nothing less!

Here are some examples that I have personally heard, and previously held as my own beliefs about money while growing up and right through to my adulthood:

"I have to work hard for my money."

"It's not fair, how come he/she can have that and not me?" "I am never going to be able to afford that."

"I am never going to have enough to buy what I like."

By holding these beliefs and mantras as your truth, it will always be your truth; nothing will change unless you start to change your

Feel Good and Watch What Happens

thinking and the words you speak. Whatever you are telling yourself becomes your truth.

You could say:

- Work is straightforward, and money flows smoothly.
- I like that car my friend bought for herself: well done to her! I know, some way or another, I will be able to get the vehicle that I like too.
- There are many different avenues that money can flow to me, and I believe I can afford anything I desire in time. I just have to ask, and I know sooner or later I will receive.

As mentioned earlier, as my children become teenagers, their choice of toys changed, they now wanted Play Stations, Nintendo, I-Phones, and all the latest technology.

I believed I was the only source to making this be their reality and would feel the pressure and knew at times I was blocking these things from being a part of our experience because of their price tags. However, in time I did buy them some of the above, and they also had lots gifted to them both.

Through my experiences, I can now recognise when I am blocking something from being part of our experience and can change in my emotions and thought process.

I have learnt how to work with my energy and slowly turn this around. I do this by saying to myself the following:

- Everything is possible. We are abundant beings.
- I am going to look for clues from the universe to bring this into our experience.
- I don't have to be the only source to where this comes from, children have asked; I know they will receive.

Anthea Morphitis

Feel Good and Watch What Happens

Think of things that are believable and resonate with you, followed by the feeling of what it feels like to receive.

For me, by thinking this way I know something will happen, and so far either another member of the family has bought it for them, extra cash has come my way, and I can buy it, or they get given money. Either way, I do my best not to allow myself to stand in the form of anything that myself or my children have asked for, and the results are phenomenal.

I now tell myself the following:

- Money loves me.
- Money flows to me.
- My money works for me and brings me more and more money
- Things come more natural and more comfortable to me.
- Life just gets better and better.
- I appreciate everything and everyone in my life
- Wellbeing is the order of my day.
- Everything is always working out for me.

I look at my children and follow their lead: children are pure positive energy and have no negative perspective on life until we implement our own beliefs in them. We are their teachers, and they are ours; they are a blessing to us, and we have been blessed to them to teach each other. Children love to have fun because they believe life is full of joy until we show them differently; they know there are no limits to growth until we teach them otherwise; children understand, when they ask it is always given.

Expect the best from your children; use positive language with them; they will get it. Extract from them all the things you like and love about them; you will always get back what you expect.

Anthea Morphitis

Feel Good and Watch What Happens

I have heard many say, and have said similar things myself like, "They're so naughty." "They never go to sleep when I tell them." Well, guess what? They won't listen and do as you ask if you don't expect them to do it.

You can choose to say:

- They are full of life and love to explore.
- Our relationship continues to improve.
- I understand my children, and they appreciate me.
- Our relationship just gets better and better. We are blessed to be in each other's lives.

Again taking your attention away from what bothers you and focusing on all the fantastic aspects of your child/children is what creates a friendly and secure relationship. Remember everything is mirroring your thoughts and emotions, especially your children. They copy what we do as we are a role model to them, and they look up to us. Their behaviour will reflect yours. Period!

When they want something, I ask them to close their eyes and imagine themselves with what they have asked for, to see themselves experiencing whatever they have expressed. To experience the feeling of having it and to know that now it's been identified, expect to receive.

It's incredible how quickly things manifest because they bring themselves to a place of believing and get excited about the feeling of having it before they have received it, seeing it as done.

When my children disagree about something, I sit back and allow them to come to their conclusion about whatever they are in disagreement about and more often than not, it will end with one of them saying "That's your perception; this is mine," and they will just get on with it.

Anthea Morphitis

Feel Good and Watch What Happens

Before we drummed our beliefs into our children and our parents drummed their views in us, we believed life is supposed to be excellent and fun. Children have a pure positive connection to who they are. It's our issues that we have experienced that change our children's perspective, and they end up thinking and believing like us, hence why so many live a similar life to what their parents lived. Break that cycle!

Now I have a different perspective I do my best to be mindful of what I say around my kids.

Their schooling has improved; they both have great relationships at school; they're both happy to wake up in the morning and attend school. They both come out of school with smiles on their faces every day, excited to tell me about their school day. When my son was not happy about attending school because he felt the teachers didn't understand him, I sat and explained that teachers are living a life just like us. They may be going through problems, so if a teacher is in a lousy mood and shouts, not to be upset or offended by it as they are just expressing how they are feeling about themselves but don't know they are doing that.

The way they communicate, it could be through shouting at their students when the student hasn't done anything, and the only reason why one student, in particular, would receive the negative attention is that they are a vibrational match to how the teacher is feeling.

They now take everything with a pinch of salt and understand that if they keep getting negative attention from particular teachers, it's because they are attracting and expecting that from the teacher and to take responsibility for the emotions and thoughts that they are feeling. They know how to see the best in people, including teachers, and can recognize why the negative attention is received. They have become good at understanding how we work and what a blessing that is at such an early stage in their life experience.

Anthea Morphitis

Feel Good and Watch What Happens

I often awaken in the morning, expecting and wondering what other pleasant surprises the universe has lined up for myself and my children. It's a bit like when we're kids at Christmas. Do you remember the excitement you felt when knowing you were going to awaken and it will be Christmas day knowing you'll be opening your presents? Well if you take every day to be Christmas day, then you can expect an abundance of gifts daily! You may not believe this to be accurate at first, but the more you practice feeling good, the better the manifestations become and will find your flow of thoughts to think to yourself that help you feel better through your day.

In my home, when the news comes on, the channel is changed, I want my children to be able to go out and not be scared and fearful of the stories they portray the world to be. If they were to listen to the news, they could very quickly tune into that fear and attract unwanted experiences.

Their minds could begin to create images which could cause them to become a vibrational match to the very thing they fear. By avoiding the news, their brains are not absorbing such negative information. Instead, we watch something that keeps smiles on our faces, knowing that when they're out of my sight, they're experiencing happy experiences.

The same goes for what is said about money, as I mentioned, up until the age of 30, I always worked for others, and I had a set amount of money coming in every month/week. My limiting belief here was that I had to work for someone to have cash flow into my life experience. A belief that I had picked up, but always knew deep down that it couldn't be true as I had seen so many others fulfil their dreams without working for someone else.

At that point, I did not have faith or belief that I could monetize the things that are of interest, and I was also unaware that I even held beliefs about myself! I thought it was reasonable to think the way I thought about me, and had no idea I could change my thinking. Once

Anthea Morphitis

Feel Good and Watch What Happens

I become aware of the Law of Attraction, I realise that there must be some sort of formula to success.

I didn't know I had to dig deep and recognise my money blockages. I realized as a kid, the word on the street was that you had to come from a wealthy background to have a university degree, be a singer, actor, doctor, to become wealthy or have businesses passed down through the family to run your own successful business.

It would have been nice if schools taught us the fact we can be, do or have anything and to follow our passion and desires; unfortunately, they teach students how to get a job and be the best candidate for that job.

Living in today's society is a blessing, as 30-odd years ago, the mindset was very different. When I spoke of creating a TV Show, the response would be, "Well, that is just a dream; this is reality" or 'Wake up and stop dreaming!' In my mind, this was crazy. Why would my mind be able to see these things if nothing could come of it? However, as it stands today, a lot more people are waking up to the fact that we create our reality, and without a dream, you will live what others expect you to live because of the beliefs embedded in you.

If you think about it, no one gets out of bed in the morning until they become conscious of getting up, and this happens via a thought. For example, the alarm goes off, and then your thought might be, "I have to get up." If the thought had not crossed your mind to get up, if we had no intention to move out of bed, then you wouldn't, right? A thought takes place first before any actions taken, and that's not just in the morning, it is with everything in life.

As I mentioned, in the past, I had always earned just about enough to get us through. I was blessed enough to have the opportunity to buy my council property when I was 25, and as a single parent, I was proud to be able to do that for myself and my children. As I

Anthea Morphitis

Feel Good and Watch What Happens

mentioned, I had often found myself in debt due to my limiting beliefs about money. I also had the opportunity to buy properties and build myself a property portfolio. Still, when I released equity from my property, I messed up due to the stress I was experiencing at the time and misused the money to buy another property. I learnt from my mistake and will not be misusing money like that again!

I got myself to a point where I would panic that I wouldn't have enough to pay the mortgage, council tax, gas, electric, ground rent, shopping, petrol—you get the picture, right? My limiting belief was that life was hard. I could not see or hear the opportunities that surrounded me.

But the reality is: life is supposed to be good. We are not here to suffer; we have the opportunity to create new beliefs, although I felt like we had at the time. When we do what we love, it does not feel like work, and money will be part of that good feeling. We are born breathing the same air; with a physical body, blood pumping round, the resources to a healthy and wealthy life are available to every single person on this planet. The key to this is your belief system, change your belief to what serves your highest good.

My limiting beliefs about money began to change when introduced to MLM (Multi-Level Marketing), which ultimately can create passive, residual income, learning all different investment strategies. I could see how easy it could be to create wealth for myself. The more focus and attention towards the above, the more people I met earning six-figure incomes and are now part of my life experience, helping me change my belief about money, and I love it!

I'm not saying that everyone wants to be wealthy, but I am saying we can have anything we desire. We just have to believe it.

I was starting to attract the life I wanted for myself and my children. My feeling good and desire to change my beliefs was paying off and meeting new people was like a breath of fresh air.

Anthea Morphitis

Feel Good and Watch What Happens

"With focus and attention, it must become"

Another example of a limiting belief that I have heard in the past is, "I can't lose weight."

If you feel you cannot do something, even if you diet, exercise or starve yourself—whatever you do, it will not work as you are telling yourselves that you can't! Now, I bet for some of you that would be a belief you would love to get rid of right?

You can learn to replace that belief: remember, you are in control of your thinking. Thought by thought, you can change your relationship with food and instead of looking at food like 'something bad' that will make you fat you can instead think of it like the petrol to your car, adding the right amount to get you through your day. If your vehicle takes petrol then I wouldn't imagine you would be feeding it, Diesel, as you know the car will not run healthy, well that's the same as your mind and body.

"Whether you think you can, or you think you can't—you're right." - Henry Ford.

I have found that using a vision board is a potent tool. By cutting out images of things that I would like to experience, buy or become and putting my attention to them, I get to experience them in time. I am not disheartened if it's yet to manifest as I said earlier, I'm not looking to eat every meal I love today, I'm happy to experience it over my lifetime.

So, if losing weight is something you would like to experience, then maybe cut out images of how you would like your body to look and feel, visualise it, feel what you believe you will feel like when you achieve it and how it will enrich your life and do this often. When we feel ready to put our weight loss into action, it will work, since you have changed your thought process towards it and believe in the actions you are taking.

Anthea Morphitis

Feel Good and Watch What Happens

You could say things like:

- My relationship with food is improving
- My body is digesting my food easier
- I'm adding the correct fuel to my body
- I feel good about the actions I'm taking

Whatever resonates with you, my suggestion is to try and make it as fun as possible for yourself, and it's not a diet, it's a new way of being, a healthy lifestyle!

It must start from within; change your story dream the dream and become the dream, imagine and feel what it would feel like to be the person you desire to be.

We have to feel it now; it's no good using the old *"I will feel good once it has happened."*

Recognise your change, celebrate every win, and be proud of all results along your way.

All the action in the world will not change anything unless you change your beliefs and how you feel. We might lose a little weight, but if we are moaning through the process and unhappy about what we are doing, then we will very quickly gain the weight back as your not working on the inner you. Once in alignment with our desire and happy with what we are doing, the weight will begin to shift as we feel better, as we will be working with inspired action instead of forced action and then the results are shown in physical form.

Ninety-nine per cent of manifestation is through though process; only 1% is the action part. Once in alignment, we will begin to experience 1%, which feels like inspired action.

An inspired action is when you fill the pull from deep within to do something, and the feeling is so strong, that if you don't do it, it just

Anthea Morphitis

Feel Good and Watch What Happens

plays on your mind until you take that action. That is your guidance system, inspiring you to take action, and that's when desire works in perfection.

As a teenager, between the ages of 14-19, I was around dressed sizes 12-14 and dreamt of being a size 8, but never believed in diets only healthy lifestyles, However, I would always exercise and loved it. I had a pretty toned body and massive boobs but wanted smaller boobs and less body. Most of my friends were tiny and everything they wore just looked good on them. There were many times when I wouldn't go to parties as I believed I looked fat and felt like crap robbing myself of experiences by staying home!

In the morning, I would feel even worse, as everyone would be talking about their night out. I remember the daydreams I would have of being a size eight and the vision of all the things I would wear. I would feel good for that moment and smile, then look at reality and feel the same before the daydream started. I didn't believe it could happen for me; told I'm heavy-boned!! And that was just the way my body was. I would moan all the time about my weight.

Well, that belief changed. My dreams then become my reality. Shortly after giving birth to my son, I become a size 8: no diets, no exercise, I just had a baby! Friends didn't recognise me; people who hadn't seen me in a while were in shock, their first question *"What did you do to lose so much weight?!"* My reply would be, *"I had a baby!"* I would often hear, *"You're so lucky!"*

At the time, I also believed I got 'Lucky'. I now understand it had nothing to do with luck; it was all that dreaming I used to do, and it had caught up with me. It no longer mattered what I would eat; I just didn't put on weight! My belief changed very rapidly, and my new belief was that I would always be a size 8! I kept this belief to be my truth by working out, eating healthy, feeling good about myself and maintain a new lifestyle.

Anthea Morphitis

Feel Good and Watch What Happens

I laugh as I now often hear, *"You're small-framed," "You are petite," "It must run in your family."* Previously, when I was heaver, it was, "Don't worry, you're just heavy boned."

By letting go of the feeling of being overweight because I was carrying a baby in my belly, I had let go of all resistance and thoughts that were stopping me from losing weight, after giving birth I was so happy that I allowed the weight to drop off. I got to wear all the clothes that I had previously seen myself to wear in my vision/dream, and it was such a good feeling. I didn't even have to try anything on; I just knew it would fit and look good on me!

When I hear others say life is hard, I interpret that as being, "I have negative thoughts going on right now, and I am attracting negative circumstances and events into my life." We become what we think!!

A belief is just a thought you keep thinking" - Abraham Hicks

Another example I could use of limiting beliefs is when you want to purchase a car. Some will purchase depending on what they believe they can afford at that particular time in their lives, looking at affordability and others will purchase what they desire, no matter the price tag; it just depends on each individual's beliefs.

When you know exactly the car we want, and you know you can afford it or you know you are abundant and don't limit yourself with price tags then, the manifestation will happen very quickly, as you are giving out a clear signal. When unsure of the type of car you want, it will take a lot longer as the signal is no longer clear, so the universe cannot deliver what you are unsure of. A thought of knowing, like 'I know I will find what I'm looking for, the universe can deliver as you KNOW what you want. A thought of doubt or confusion like 'I don't know what car I want,' or 'All the cars I like

Anthea Morphitis

Feel Good and Watch What Happens

are too expensive,' and the universe cannot deliver a car as the signal is unclear. It is your thought and feeling process that determines how fast or how slow things manifest for you. It is the feeling that brings the manifestation, the feeling creates the manifestation, and so by feeling positive and joyful, you give out good feeling vibes which are followed by good feeling thoughts. So thoughts and vision are more likely to be of one, then you realise the exact car for you and drive away in the car you KNEW you wanted.

The surroundings that surround us and what we observe every day is what keeps us believing what we believe to be the truth about who we are, and what we will become in our future experience.

As I have mentioned, until the age of 7, my family lived in a three-bedroom house with beautiful surroundings. All our neighbours lived good, healthy and abundant lives. Most were married with children, owned their businesses, drove beautiful cars and often took holidays. Naturally, I believed at the time that this was what life was about and desired to have the same.

When my parents split, it messed with my dreams and beliefs; I seemed to have gone from abundance to not enough. I remember everyone around me looked sad, would complain of not enough money, buying a car was an issue, and those who did have cars struggled to maintain them, completely the opposite of what I had known.

When we moved to the estate, my beliefs began to change to the same as my surroundings, and I remember thinking that this was not going to set me on a soundtrack. My mum was on income support, there never seemed to be enough money flowing around, and the language in our home was always of negative words.

My beliefs about having a family, being abundant and wealthy slowly changed, as I was always told, "I can't afford it." That was all I heard, so that's what I believed and become my dominate thoughts.

Anthea Morphitis

Feel Good and Watch What Happens

My beliefs changed from believing I could pretty much have anything I wanted in life to believing life was hard. I felt insecure, unworthy and life is hard.

Limiting ourselves with our thoughts will create feelings that do not resonate with our natural wellbeing, when, in fact, there is no reason why we cannot live a life of freedom and abundance. The only reason why people hold back from what they really would like to do is that they don't believe in themselves; hence, people live a life of unhappiness, holding onto relationships and jobs that don't serve them. It doesn't work out for them; they give up at the first hurdle.

You are giving yourself reasons why you can't only hold you back from having the very thing that you want. You must change your inside story, look forward to experiencing the things you want by finding reasons why. Stop thinking of the hows and think of the whys instead. So what harm will it do to expect the best in your life?? No harm whatsoever!!! What harm will it do to expect the worst??? Lots!!!!

I've often heard the question," If we're supposed to live a good life, why is there poverty in the world? Why are there starving children?" My reply, because they don't expect to live well, from the time they're born, it is programmed in them, the lack, they are not programmed to believe you can be anything you want, or you can achieve your dreams. There is no visual to a good life, no awareness of living well, so how can anyone experience what they don't expect? You live what you expect. Some just know in there heart and soul that there is more to life and eventually leave to see what the world has to offer.

Just writing this book causes a good feeling for me as I know I am raising awareness, and it's up to each individual who reads this as to what they get out of it.

Anthea Morphitis

Feel Good and Watch What Happens

I can write book after book, and read book after book, but the bottom line is that it is up to me what I choose to do with the information I have heard or read. I believe words don't teach; it is the life experience that teaches. However, through experience, the words that we read can fit in like a puzzle experiencing those 'AHAA! Moments'

Experiences that most here in the UK expect to live daily; like eating are ones that someone living in poverty may not expect.

The reason why people in poverty may not expect it is because it's never been part of their experience to believe they can have it. Just like everything I have spoken about thus far, someone who lives in poverty will have a completely different perspective on life than someone who lives an abundant life.

I watched a cool documentary on YouTube last night, about the Billionaires' lifestyle; it was amazing!! Their private jets, ten-bed homes, helicopters and yachts, just to name a few. They could buy whatever they wanted; there was no limit to what they can have. I loved every minute of the programme. It showed me that you really could be, do or have anything we desire.

There are only 1342 billionaires in this world, and the United States claims 442 of them. My perspective is that they just understand how to align themselves with their desires; they believe in themselves and their wellbeing. It#s not likely to hear someone successful say, "I can't." They know they can have anything they want and will overcome any obstacle that may be in their way.

We can see how that belief and thought process has served them well in their lives. It was fascinating, as a few of the billionaires had come from poverty and had expressed that they had had enough of living that way and decided to go on a rampage of finding ways to better their lifestyle, and boy did they do that! I felt so inspired; it would be nice to be part of that Billionaire club. Bring it on!!!

Anthea Morphitis

Feel Good and Watch What Happens

Like I said earlier, we tend to use our surroundings to create our beliefs about what we can and cannot have. People who do not live their passions just don't know any different; opportunities may be there but not realized, stopping them from moving forward.

How can we experience different from what we are currently living?? By digging deep and finding the blockages caused by childhood and understanding that everyone experiences fear even successful people but the reason why they have become successful is that they felt the fear and done it anyway. Don't let fear hold you. Change your thought patterns: we live what we think. The people who have broken through their thought patterns of poverty now live a completely different lifestyle to what they lived as kids.

Often people who have broken through their poverty barrier become a blessing in society, by openly giving to charities and or starting charities of their own.

I love it when I see or hear people who have helped create a better education system, spent time with children in poverty to guide them in believing in themselves. Helping create more success stories, and the more success stories there are, the more people will believe in changing the way they think and feel, and the better all round.

If you were to be stranded on an island and focused on lack of food, you would probably find it hard to survive. On the other hand, if you were to focus on how much fresh food you could experience while there, you would be more likely to eat well. Your instincts would guide you to the fruit trees and whatever food an island could offer. We simply get what we think and expect.

Just as I was writing this, I received a phone call from an unknown number, I answered the call, and blow me down, it was a friend that I had thought of this morning, I had had a bit of a daydream about seeing him. I thought how nice it would be if we spoke, and within hours we spoke, Law of Attraction in action.

Anthea Morphitis

Feel Good and Watch What Happens

I love it!!!! Thoughts are shown to you 24/7, whether you are aware or not.

"Failure is the opportunity to begin again more intelligently." - Henry Ford

Anthea Morphitis

Chapter 17: Is There a Limit for What I Can Manifest?

So now you understand limiting beliefs, and if everything is ENERGY, including humans, and everything works from an energy frequency in alignment to the signals that we are sending out to the universe. We receive what we are thinking and feeling 24 hours a day, seven days a week, then think about this:

Is there a difference between a Beef Burger and a Ferrari???

Let me answer that; The answer is NO!!!!

There is absolutely no difference between the two; they are both made up of energy. It is just what the eyes perceive it to be, and there is no difference!!!

The only reason why we see them be different is because of the price tag. A Ferrari, as you know, could cost anything in the price range of thousands and a burger could cost under £1; therefore, the belief system will determine whether you buy burgers whenever you want, Ferrari's or both!! A bit like the Billionaires who believe they could buy 20 Ferraris if desired.

Now, this is where the belief system comes into play. When you look at a Ferrari, you may think to yourself, "Wow, I would love to have one of them," but automatically your thought process could be, I will never afford it due to the price. You may see others driving one and think that person is so lucky, but you are just as lucky as they are; they were not born with any more luck than you were. Just wanted to add, there is a restaurant in America that sells burgers for $350.00! So it comes back to the story you tell yourself, the thoughts you think and the perception you have.

When the BMW X5 first was introduced, I fell in love with it, every time I would see one, I would say 'that's mine'.

Anthea Morphitis

Feel Good and Watch What Happens

My son even made me a card, and on the front, he drew a picture of an X5 and wrote inside the card ` To Mummy, I promise you when I get big I will buy you this` I love him so much, anyway my point is, I spent hours daydreaming and talking about having one. I would imagine myself driving it, believed I had it. I would visualise the car outside my home and just knew it would be mine to experience.

Within a few months, I was out with a friend and decided to stop at a car showroom just for fun, as I pulled up in my little Fiat Punto an X5 had just arrived into the showroom, my heart was beating with excitement, I asked to test drive it, and within a couple of hours, it was mine. Happy days my son cried from happiness and then asked *"What car do I buy you now, mummy?"* bless him.

Remember, if everything is energy and wherever we choose to put our focus and attention to, wanted or unwanted, with pure belief, then it must manifest. It's up to you what you experience. Take the money out of the equation, think of your desires as energy, and ask yourself what energy am I giving out?, am I expecting to experience this or not? Am I focusing on the absence of it or the feeling of having it?

Most do not think twice about passing through a fast food restaurant at any time of the day as they believe they can afford it. You do this subconsciously; you probably don't stop and think, "I would love a burger, but I can't afford it." You are more likely to go and buy one!!

So you expect to be able to walk into a fast-food restaurant and order a burger at any time and pay for it, however passing by a car showroom that sells Ferraris, could be a different story! You may not hold the same belief system as you do about eating. You may just look and wish, maybe imagine for a minute what it would feel like, but once you walk away, you probably forget about it.

So many have picked up so many limiting beliefs about themselves along with their experience that they find themselves struggling every day, maybe even with food shopping!!!

Anthea Morphitis

Feel Good and Watch What Happens

Well, one of my newfound beliefs is that everyone deserves a good life experience. I don't care what your name is, where you are from and who you think you are, no one is more worthy than anyone else, we create our luck, and through thoughts a path to anything you want becomes apparent.

I believe there is no better time than the present to start working on your belief system a thinking mechanism that creates results daily, and I don't just mean physical results I also mean emotional.

As Abraham Hicks says, *"It's as easy to create a castle as it is to create a button"* People focus on £10 an hour receive £10 an hour, the people who focus on residual income, receive residual income. It's not because one person's job is more worthy than another; it's purely where the individual is focused. Expect wealth, and in time you will experience wealth, ways realized by you to create wealth in your experience. Expect poverty, and you will experience poverty!

Once we begin to expect to live well, taking limitations out the equation, believing and expecting to receive the best in life, then whether it is a Ferrari or a burger, it makes no difference as long as we believe and expect, then it must be.

There is no limit to what we can have and experience. We may have the heard the saying 'the sky is the limit.' Well, I don't even believe that; I believe the limit is eternal unless you give yourself a limit.

Fear will hold you back. Let go and live life; do everything you have said you want to do. Feel the fear and take that leap. Fear is False Evidence Appearing Real.

Breaking free of negative thoughts is a process, just like learning to drive. It's a process that begins with a thought and an intention; the first thought could be "Wouldn't it be nice to learn to drive?" followed by different emotions, maybe you feel apprehensive or even fearful, thinking, "what if, I never get the hang of driving"? Anyway, after talking to a few friends, you begin to feel a little more excited

Anthea Morphitis

Feel Good and Watch What Happens

about the idea of learning to drive and naturally create images in your mind of the experience. By taking the steps towards learning to drive you will slowly get over the fear as I said, Personal Development teaches to feel the fear and do it anyway, and by taking the first lesson, you will find that it's not as scary as you thought!

Depending on the thought process in between, will also determine how long it takes for you to pass your test. Feeling like you're not good enough at driving will prolong the results and so will being fearful that you won't pass. With an attitude of knowing, looking forward, seeing yourselves pass, feeling what it feels like to drive your own car, imagining the places you will go and feeling the feeling of that, then the results will become sooner rather than later.

We are sending signals out to the universe with pure power and believe that the universe then begins to move circumstances and events to make it be. Many will hold the examiner responsible for the outcome on the day and blame him for failing the test.

I've heard things like, "Hopefully I get, a friendly examiner and I pass my driving test.

I'm excited, and I look forward to driving my car.

The two examples above are more likely to result in a driving licence.

And you have the other side of the spectrum when someone say's

I don't think I'm going to pass!

I'm scared, what if I mess up badly?!" the latter is more likely to result in a fail. And often blame the examiner! expressing "His so out of order!" Blaming and holding others responsible for what they are aligning with, always be aware of what your language, thoughts and emotions are limning you up with, allowing fear and negative talk to dominate your desire, then the desire cannot be.

Anthea Morphitis

Feel Good and Watch What Happens

The signal we are sending out is of fear and failure, which attracts like for like circumstances. What others express about their beliefs does not have to be your belief; it is up to you to align yourself with the outcome.

Fearing the unknown will stop you living an abundant life that you know you deserve.

Keep in mind that everything is always working out for you and keep a positive attitude, knowing what you want will be.

Being able to hold a dominant thought of success, overpowering the fear of failure, being in a state of feeling good and positive thoughts creates alignment with the universe with the things you want. Resulting in you being a fully-fledged legal driver and enjoying the freedom of driving or whatever the desire.

You just didn't realise throughout the entire process that everything is aligning according to your thought process, and I mean everything. From the driving instructor you choose, the car you learnt in, the number of lessons you took, the date and time you took your test to the examiner that either passed you are not! Everything you experienced was a part of the process to achieving your licence and like I said the universe aligns with you either which way rounds. It was not a matter of thinking licence, and the licence just appeared: there was a process that you experienced. The same applies when becoming aware of your thoughts and emotions. Taking your thoughts from negative to positive; feeling insecure to secure, from fearful to fearless. It is unlikely that we will make this happen overnight.

Whatever is going on in your lives right now, it's only for now, and you have the power to change your life. It is time to take control and stop letting fear stop you. Do you think that I've had no fear in writing this book? I was scared, shitless! Scared of being judged, scared of what family would say, but you know what, I felt the fear

Anthea Morphitis

and still took the steps towards writing this book because I knew that this book is not for my ego. It's to help others alike get to grips with who they are and the beautiful things that can achieve in life when we forgive, love thyself and do what feels right for us; then the universe will gift us with our desires.

We deserve a good life, right? The first step is to become aware of our thoughts, and it really does not matter how long it takes. Time will pass regardless, so holding an awareness of how you feel most of the time will always help you along with the process. You can get past anything when you put your minds to it.

I know when I felt my relationship with my ex-boyfriend had run its course, I feared to be alone, knowing that I would put my children to bed in the evening and have no one to interact with scared me. Once I made my decision, I was so surprised how much I loved my own company.

My life becomes mine again, and I had time to get to know me and what I wanted, allowing me to be Anthea! It was one of the best decisions I could have made at that point in my life.

"Say bye to the past life of what you don't want and say hi to a new-found life of what you do want"

Be easy on yourself in the process, and there is no need to mentally beat yourself up when you are feeling low, at least you are aware, and you can do something about it, imagine when you weren't aware, and you felt low, that feeling and trail of thought could go on for months! Beginning a momentum of negative thoughts, attracting more of the same in future circumstances and events, and now you know different.

Working with this process, I always think it's a good idea to ask asking yourself questions and an even better idea to stand in front of a mirror when asking, Ask yourself, "What would happen if I left the

Feel Good and Watch What Happens

fear of not succeeding behind me?" When we ask, we receive the answer. We just need to listen to it.

Starting a process of making fear the friend, not the enemy, finding solutions that you can believe. Knowing everything will always work out, leaving the past to rest and enjoying the Now; leaving the problem to only be seen in the rear-view mirror, jumping in the front seat, looking forward, allowing the solution to become the new focus.

When getting into your car to go on a long journey and along your journey, you take a wrong turn and find yourselves lost, I wouldn't stop at that point and say I am turning around and heading home just because I took a wrong turn; I don't believe anyone would. Just like myself, I believe you would ask people to help you get back on track. There will always be bumps in the road of life, and we have to overcome them to get back on track.

When consciously going from negative to positive, we begin to see and feel how the law of attraction works, continually reminding us that we are the creators of our reality. As long as we take note of the way things are changing for us and appreciate every step of the way, slowly but surely we can re-create, leaving fear to be the past and creating a future of freedom.

The same applies to everything. When we are feeling, seeing, knowing, believing and expecting before we physically see something, then it must be as we expected it to be. For example, I have heard many successful singers/artists say, "I just knew that's what I wanted to do in my life." They held a vision, believing in their desire, followed their passion, and they knew it was the right path for them.

Most don't know how they did it; they just could see themselves on stage performing, and didn't give up; they stayed focused on their desire. Knowing singing feels good, When a singer proforms they are at their happiest, and their frequency is high and tuned in, they

Anthea Morphitis

Feel Good and Watch What Happens

are sending out signals of happiness to the universe. Once they are in pure belief of themselves, they become aligned with the universe, and the manifestation takes place. They then begin living life as they see it to be.

Their vision manifests; they then become artists just as they expected. Some become famous world-renowned singers. They thrive, with downloads, record sales, thousands of views on YouTube, TV interviews; just thriving with all the positive energy that projected out.

The artists receive all circumstances and events to make this be. They may have started to create at a young age or later on in life; either way, they live what they expect and more. Paths open in every direction; they create every day what makes them feel good. In this example, Singing! Energy is flowing, they plan forward to creating the next single, plan for concerts, realise dates. The artists are receiving what they are thinking and feeling. They love to sing and perform. You may have even heard yourself of singers saying, "Singing is all I think about".

There are a few friends of mine who are now living their passions and dreams, one who fits into this example has been songwriting for several years; he refused to give up on himself and has recently signed to a record label working with very well-known artists.

Now, he could have given up and said it was a waste of time because he wasn't getting the result he wanted. However, he didn't; he kept his faith and belief in his passion, believing in his ability to write good music. He writes with passion and loves what he does, and now paid for his efforts. Prepared to stick to his passion, whether paid or not and now it has paid off.

Secondly, his girlfriend, a long-time friend of mine who introduced me to Abraham Hick's teachings, also wanted to open and run her own advanced beauty clinic. She had spoken of this from when we

Anthea Morphitis

Feel Good and Watch What Happens

were teenagers, and with her passion and belief, she has just signed the paperwork to get her business having her shopfront.

Thirdly a good female friend of mine who is a hairstylist was handpicked panel of professional after entering a completion and won the opportunity to work as an international hairstylist, styling celebrity's hair at the London 2012 Olympics.

Well done to you all. I love it. I am very proud to be part of your growth and journey. You all looked forward with passion, believed in yourself and held faith, knowing you are good at what you do, being a good example and walked in the direction of your dream which has now lead to becoming your reality just as you knew it would.

I was cleaning my house yesterday and noticed every little detail in my home. I paused for a minute, just taking in the content of my home, appreciating all that I have attracted into my life, and I suddenly realised that every single thing is a creation of someone's thoughts. Wow!

Now that realisation did bring a smile to my face. I looked over at my fridge freezer and thought, Someone had an idea to keep food chilled and stored at a particular coolant level so food can last longer.

They believed in their thoughts and ideas, assuming they became excited about what they were thinking, began putting thoughts to paper, expanding on the idea and slowly but surely from a thought, it started to become their reality and visible to others. Now millions of people around the world have a fridge/freezer.

How cool is that! Everything starts with thoughts/idea cars, sofas to knives and forks to aeroplanes, so why not add to that the expansion of the universe and believe in your thoughts and ideas. If everything begins with a thought and all these people have had success, so can you! There is absolutely no reason why it can't be one of us who proposes the next idea out there, especially in this day and age. There

Anthea Morphitis

Feel Good and Watch What Happens

is so much support for new ideas. So many people bypass their ideas because they think it's a silly idea; however, someone who works with ideas daily may see the potential and want to work with you. Even if we are turned down by one, it does not mean your idea is not valid.

Look at J.K Rowling, her pitch for Harry Potter rejected 12 times, and now a world-renowned success!

The manifestation of "YOUR" Thoughts From the "UNREAL" to the "REAL"!

First, we have a burst of inspiration, IDEA or Thought

i. Then we "FEEL" the goosebumps or Emotions attached to this Inspiration

ii. Then we take Actions, meaning our Emotions have now become active or "IN MOTION", thus Energy in motion, and as we Move or ARE IN MOTION, we create FORCE. As movement occurs, it causes unseen Atomic Particles to Magnetically "ATTRACT" to our Holographic IMAGE or IMAGES, Magnetic Attraction and FORCE = LAW OF ATTRACTION.

iii. We then begin to see the manifestation in the three solid visible realities as Persons we will ATTRACT to assist us into bringing this IDEA INTO SOLID REALITY,

iv. Places that we might go to bring this IDEA into Solid Reality, or things we might need to acquire to bring this Thought, IDEA, or Inspiration into Solid Reality = MANIFESTATION OF THOUGHTS!

Anthea Morphitis

Chapter 18: Believing In My Ideas

A great example of what I was just talking about in the last chapter. About a year and a half ago, I had an idea to produce a T.V show; I thought the concept was great; however, I didn't believe I could make it happen! Self-doubt will often stop you from doing what you want. After pondering on the idea, the excitement kicked in, visuals forming in my mind's eye, it took me all this time to gain the confidence to express my idea. I was working with people who inspired me daily, and hearing them express there dreams and desires allowed me to do the same.

The inspiration of the producing a TV show mostly came from working in the network marketing world, listening to motivational speakers, building relationships with great and like-minded people and watching how they prospered in their everyday lives.

I was meeting people in the property and investment industries, showing me I had changed my point of attraction. I was witnessing first-hand the concept of 'Ask, and it's Given'. Some of these people started their 'New' journeys with a vast amount of debt; however, by consistently attending seminars, listening to others who were now thriving in their lives and learning new ways of being and thinking become financially free!! Some had already become millionaires, and you could feel and see how happy and grateful they are, teaching others how they aligned with there purpose and living a fulfilling life.

If they can do it, you can too!

One friend in particular that I mentioned earlier, who is a semi-professional footballer, has always inspired me. We met at an event and at just 22 years old, he has his investment hat on, building his empire and knowing what he wants to achieve in life. He knows his why's and works towards them daily.

Feel Good and Watch What Happens

As I was saying regarding creating a show, the more focus I am putting towards it the right people are showing up willing and eager to be a part of it. The feedback is phenomenal; others are now excited about it coming together. Many are in support of my idea, offering their help and support; it is coming together in the best way possible. I am loving how the universe works and having so much fun every day proving my worthiness to myself and how easy it is to create a better life just by focusing on the things that cause me to feel good and riding the waves of good feelings. I love every second of this new chapter in my life and have just recently had a meeting regarding the show. I have built a team; we are soon ready to apply for funding and look forward to what's next.

A couple of days after writing the above paragraph, while at work in a well-known shopping centre, a very successful investor walked past me. My friend and I looked at one another and said: *"Is that the guy from the program Dragon's Den!?"* OMG, it is! Wow, my first thought was "I can't let him walk past and not take this opportunity". I grabbed my friend's arm and said: *"You're coming with me!"* We started running towards him; my heart was beating 10 to the dozen. I shouted his name, he stopped, turned and said "Hi" so I introduced myself *"Hi. My name is Anthea nice to meet you."*

"Nice to meet you too" he replied. We shook hands and had a little conversation about my project. He asked me to send him an email explaining what I was doing. I felt like the most potent being at that point, amazing. One minute I am asking for an investor, and the next I meet the best I could have met. I was so excited and still am. This shit works, trust me, defining what you want and taking the necessary actions towards it daily with a positive attitude, you will be surprised and delighted by what starts to happen!

Life is a journey; we have to experience what we don't want so we can become clear of what we do want. Think back to some of your experiences for a minute or two, if you didn't experience them, would you know that you didn't want to experience them again? And

Anthea Morphitis

Feel Good and Watch What Happens

what you would like instead? Would you want what you want now without those

experiences? If you have experienced unfilling relationships, then you know you now want to experience fulfilling ones instead. Right?

A few weeks before moving to mum's again, I had said to a friend that I would like to find work that enabled me to choose my hours, meet new people and have fun.

A few days had passed by since expressing my thoughts, it was midnight, and a friend and I were relaxing watching a film.

My friend received a call; it was her friend who was working for a promotional company offering her a promotional offer for a newspaper. She rolled her eyes, passing the phone to me and said, *"Here, babe, take the call. I'm not interested, but I know you will be."*

"Her friend explained the offer; without hesitation, I signed up. I then asked, "How did you get this work?"

"Why, are you interested?"

"Yes!!" I replied, *"It sounds easy and fun!"*

He went on to explain what the job entailed and was what I had voiced a few days prior. Within three days, I was working for the same company.

My sales were sky high, and the money was rolling in, and I was having so much fun! Oh, yeah! Self-employed, choosing the number of days I wanted to work. Ninety-five per cent of my colleagues were actors/actresses, singers and dancers and to top it all off we had a stand, at Stratford's Westfield's shopping centre during the 2012 Olympics.

Anthea Morphitis

Feel Good and Watch What Happens

The atmosphere daily was buzzing; the energy was high and full of positive vibes. My children would often say they had never met anyone that wanted to go to work as much as I did. I looked forward to every day, meeting coaches of the athletes, the athletes and just great and inspiring people, enjoying the most stimulating conversations, laughing, joking all day and making some good money.

Who would not love going to work?! Due to my constant desire to be happy and feeling good; my path was becoming more transparent. I had asked for work that enabled me to choose my hours to meet new people and have fun, and that is what I received.

My daughter recently said that she had read a quote saying, "When you do what you love to do, then you never have to work a day in your life."

I was meeting so many new people every day, building relationships with new colleagues, security guards, police and life was and still is just buzzing.

After a while of working, I decided to go on holiday with my children. While abroad, early August 2012, I began to receive unpleasant text messages from my daughter's father, as soon as I read the first text, I knew he was facing some challenging issues. He began by threatening to take me to court again, wanting to have custody of our daughter. The letters from the solicitors started rolling in again.

Any text that I had read was just a reflection of how he was feeling about himself. He didn't know what to do with his negative feelings and thoughts and thought he would put them on me as it was so easy to blame me and that's just what he was used to doing. It also meant that he didn't have to take responsibility for what was going wrong in his life. He is unaware that I understand and practice the Law of

Anthea Morphitis

Feel Good and Watch What Happens

Attraction, and I am very good at analysing each situation as to why it is happening.

I took no offence to it and completely ignored every text and phone call I received. I waited a while, and through the grapevine, I heard everything that he was experiencing, and guess what: the texts mirrored his mental and emotional state.

I carried on, trying not to allow outside circumstances affect my happiness. Within a few weeks; I received a text explaining how proud he felt of my progress!

Wow, now there's a turnaround from just two months prior. I paid absolutely no attention to the negative words and emotions that I was receiving, kept my thoughts to be of appreciation and love towards him. Therefore, cut the energy flow off, meaning the energy could not be part of my experience. The result was love and appreciation towards me—just my mirror reflection of my thoughts and feelings about him.

I am so happy that I know what I know, and I am not drawn into all of that anymore. I can allow myself to be the best I can be with pure love, not allowing other's insecurities and surroundings to determine my happiness in each living moment.

On our return from our holiday, I headed straight back to work, knowing the next thing on my list was to align myself with my desire of moving into our own home. A couple of months passed by, and I was feeling better by the second. I had been out with my sister one particular morning; we had visited a friend of hers, and while there, we had a conversation about moving into a home, and she recommended an estate agent that she had used to get her property. After leaving, I began my journey home.

I intended to get a bus; however, my phone rang, and I was engaged in deep conversation. And before I knew it, I had walked a fair bit of my journey, stopped in mid-conversation and as I turned to my left,

Anthea Morphitis

Feel Good and Watch What Happens

I was standing in front of the estate agent's that she recommended, and my heart was pulsing with excitement.

Wow! I popped my head in, asked if they had any three-bedroom properties in Cheshunt (the agency was in Enfield) and they replied;

"Not typically, but this must be your lucky day as we have just put the phone down to a client who would like to let his property in Cheshunt. When are you free for a viewing?" OMG, the universe is fantastic.

Wow, I was so excited after viewing the property! I just knew it was for us. The landlord had asked to meet me, so I went round after work one day and the second he opened the door, we had a great connection. We sat and spoke for an hour, laughing and joking, and we both walked away with big smiles on our faces.

Everything came together in such an easy and digestible way; I kept my faith and belief, knowing we deserved our home. I had also spent a lot of time visualizing, feeling the feeling of being in our home. The children and I had many conversations about their friends coming to stay, planning our housewarming party.

As far as we were concerned, it had already happened. We planned the decorations we would be buying for Christmas, we chose our Christmas tree, and we just knew we would be waking up in our home on Christmas day.

I would often drive, imaging I was driving to my home. I changed my language to one of the presents, without feeling like it was missing in our lives. I became the experience before it happened, and then it happened!

A delightful turnaround from only seven months prior when we did not have a stable home, with minimal contact with my children.

Anthea Morphitis

Feel Good and Watch What Happens

"Love who you are; love every moment of your life, even the people who you feel upset you or bring you down, as these are the people who help you pick out with a fine-tooth comb what you want" - *Anthea Morphitis*

You are where we are, find things to love about where you are. You don't need to be anywhere other than where you are to be happy with the person you are. You are worth everything, We are living this life for a reason, and the reason is joy and fulfilment, and you bring value to the world whether you know it or not! You only need you to be happy, and the rest will follow!

Get excited and look forward to whats next, imagine, daydream away, feel the feeling, get excited, and become the very thing we want.

We can BE, DO or HAVE ANYTHING we desire. The key is to FEEL GOOD AND APPRECIATE!! Get out your way and certainly don't allow others opinions to stand in your way; if someone has a problem with your dreams and desires, just know it's their problem, not yours! Be the best version of you!

Bless every situation as each experience ties into the journey of what you would like to experience, and there is always something more significant then what you are currently living.

We are continually shooting out rockets of desires; whether it's something in particular that we fancy having for dinner or we fancy going for a drive; whatever it is, we are asking all day every day. Think about it: why do you want anything? It's for the feeling, eating food that we love, the reason we love it is because of the feeling it brings us while eating it: the taste, the smell and so forth.

The same applies to anything. I love fast cars: the reason why I love them is because of the feeling I get from driving them—the exhilaration, my heart pumping, the goosebumps running through my body and the sound of the engine. I love it.

Anthea Morphitis

Feel Good and Watch What Happens

Well, it is time to start believing in what you would like to experience! I don't care what it is; all I know is that you can have it, as long as you drop any excuses to why you can't and find every reason to why you can, the path will light up

While writing this, I received my mail and guess what: I received a cheque for £800, the exact amount that I had asked for recently. Again, I felt like it had already happened, by letting go and knowing it would be, I received. Love it!

The main things to do to help you feel good:

If you are not happy within yourselves, you're going to have a tough time achieving in life. As you may be aware, the main point I am highlighting in this book is that anyone can change their lives for the better.

We have the choice in the thoughts we think, and WE SHOULD NOT LET THEM CONTROL US. Although this can feel hard at times—I know from personal experience—but every human was born with the same powers. Unfortunately, we are programmed to believe that we have to work hard for money to flow and life is supposed to be hard, and these beliefs continue to keep people feeling very LIMITED to what they can achieve. It's time to take your god-given rights and powers back and believe you can achieve anything you put your mind too!

DO:

Do Smile as much as possible; it's easier than you think.

Do Start your morning by appreciating yourself and your surroundings; it's easier than you think.

Do practice meditation.

Be happy with where you currently stand in life as you are where you are!

Anthea Morphitis

Feel Good and Watch What Happens

Do stand up straight and feel proud.

Do Read daily to expand on your knowledge, ideas and imagination.

Do get clear on how you would like to live your life.

Do write a list of all that you appreciate.

Do Watch programs that are inspiring to you.

Do Listen to calming music.

Do dress well; clothing can help you feel good.

Do connect with new and positive people.

Do speak of the things you are looking forward to experiencing.

Do take full responsibility for how you feel at all times.

Anthea Morphitis

Chapter 19: Faith

My definition of faith is 'Beliving before Receiving' knowing that I will receive without needing the evidence to believe! No doubt, just knowing and expecting it to be.

> *"Faith is taking the first step, even when you don't see the whole staircase."- Martin Luther King, Jr.*

Faith! Just recently, my children, sister and I had been reminiscing about my ex-partner that I briefly spoke about at the beginning of this book, and haven't communicated since the relationship ended in 2009.

We had been talking about all the good times we experienced with him which got me thinking how nice it would be to talk to him again, as every time the conversation involved his name, we all had smiles on our faces.

I started to search online for a way to contact him. I then stopped and thought to myself, "I have asked for contact, so it must be! Within two weeks, I received an e-mail from him! Yes! It's as easy as that!

I had faith; I had no idea how. I just knew that I had asked for contact and it had to be.

I didn't question anything. I just had the thought that it would be nice if we spoke again, and allowed that thought to be, and it was great to catch up and communicate how we felt, allowing us both to have positive closure. I felt the power within me and knew the communication would be excellent for us.

> *"Life will always throw things your way. We live in a contrasting world; it is up to you how you choose to feel about it and whether you have faith that things are always working out for you."*

Anthea Morphitis

Feel Good and Watch What Happens

Keeping and having faith in what you have asked for will change your life experience. You deserve the best, so do your children, families and friends.

Life will test you and push you to your limits but without faith and belief that you will get through it, then where does that leave you?

Here's another recent experience of faith that I experienced recently. I had to attend court in mid-January 2013 as there had been some confusion that somehow involved my name as soon as I heard about it, I knew it had nothing to do with me and asked if I could go to court to have my say.

A date set for me to attend court, however, I happened to be working that particular day. I was working in Wandsworth, which is about a 2-hour train journey for me and the court I had to attend was only two train stops away. I mean, what can I say, I'm lucky or is it the fact that everything is always working out! I used my lunch break to attend court as I had already decided I would be back within the hour. I knew I had done nothing wrong and had prepared how I wanted the case to work out for me and considered it a done deal. I knew I would be seen and heard straight away and that there would be no waiting around.

I arrived and seen within five minutes—as I knew I would be—and to top it off, I also had a fantastic time. I gave my name, swore the oath, and the case began. A lady stood up (I had no idea that she even existed) and just started defending me. It was crazy; she had so much character and charisma. I felt like an angel had landed.

As the judges left the courtroom to make their decision, the remaining people in the courtroom was the lady who was defending me, the usher, the opposition and me. The conversation between us all was just flowing, they were speaking about a TV show that they all recently watched and loved, and how after work they'd all be going out to get drunk, a bunch of happy, joyful, full of stories and

Anthea Morphitis

Feel Good and Watch What Happens

laughter. I felt like it was a dream; I was in the middle of a courtroom, and happy to be there, with these great and charismatic people.

The three judges re-entered the room, and said, "We find you not guilty. You are free to go!"

I had held my belief and knew I would be ok, and I believed everything would work out and had already heard what I expected the Judge to say "Not Guilty, You are free to go" That's what it was.

I was back to work within the hour, just as I knew I would be. These types of experiences prove to me that as long as I'm loyal to myself and I know in my heart of hearts that I have nothing to hide I feel good, trust in myself knowing that everything is always working out for not just me but everybody then life can flow well.

> *"Believe in what's real to you; faith is a powerful tool to have within."*

Anthea Morphitis

Chapter 20: Relationships

Talking about faith comes relationships. First and foremost, the most crucial relationship is the relationship you have with you. Unfortunately, so many people rely on another to make them happy and put the other first thinking they can make them happy!

People tend to start a relationship in the best way possible and quickly get themselves into a habit of expecting the other to behave in ways that they deem right!

We often begin a relationship with a positive outlook, emotions of excitement, focusing on all the positive aspects and loving everything about them, focusing on all the things we like, feeling happy until they do something we don't like! Most call this the honeymoon period.

Many start a relationship looking for love in all the wrong places. What do I mean by this? We often don't fill up our cup before we get together, holding another responsible for our happiness; this does not work. As discussed throughout this book, only you can make yourself happy. The other person is there as a reflection of who you are and how you feel. The breakdown of a relationship happens when the focus becomes negative, forgetting the reason why you was attracted to the relationship in the first place.

Too many people set unrealistic expectations and holding their partner responsible for their sense of security. Too often, we stop doing what we love to suit another, and this also doesn't work. One may express that they do not want their partner to go on holiday with the boys/girls, It is not your choice, it's up to your partner, just because you are in a relationship, it does not give you the right to limit someone's experiences because you feel insecure. Insecurity will create thoughts that will not serve either of you.

Anthea Morphitis

Feel Good and Watch What Happens

Again this comes back to trust or faith in you or shall I say lack of it.

I will say both and let me answer why I believe this to be.

You have to respect you first, know that you are worthy of living the best version of you regardless of what the other is doing, staying true to yourself by not doing things that you think will make the other person like you more. Be you!

Once you are happy with you, then you can have a meaningful relationship with another, knowing that if you don't agree on something, you can communicate the problem and search for the solution together. Entering a relationship because you think that the person can make you happy is the wrong way round, People have a habit of holding on to another because they are frightened to be alone, even though we are born naked and alone!

I also believe men seek freedom and women seek security.

Being in a relationship and holding your partner hostage for the way you feel is a big responsibility for your partner. Would you agree?

I have previously done this myself where I notice things that bug me, putting my focus there, slowly, forgetting all the reasons why we were attracted to each other in the first place—then blaming my partner for the way I feel.

Remember where attention goes, energy flows and grows. So, as I've mentioned The Law of Attraction reflect how you are thinking and feeling. The arguments start, and the blame goes from one to the other, and before you know it, the relationship is breaking down.

Instead, the best way to keep a relationship alive is to focus on feeling good by filling up your cup with happy thoughts and doing the things you love to do regardless of the other person.

Anthea Morphitis

Feel Good and Watch What Happens

By entering into the relationship to enhance your happiness—not because you feel you need to have someone in your life but because it is nice to have someone to love and share the fun of life with—then things that may class as faults in your eyes wouldn't bother you, as you are happy and are to busy focusing on all the good things about you and your relationship to think about little things that really don't matter!

It would serve you so much better to focus on the positive aspects of your partner or any relationship; it all goes back to caring more about how you feel rather than what another is thinking or feeling. When two people come together, who both care more about how they feel rather then what the other is thinking, then your journey together would flow with positive intent.

As I said, it works for me, and others that I know who had "problems" in their relationships, after speaking to friends and explaining what is happening due to the attention that on the problem, the problem keeps expanding.

A friend tried this by redirecting her attention from the things that bothered her and focused on appreciating the things she can love about him.

The attention shifted from problem to appreciation, and he had no idea of what she did, but said to her, "We get on well now, don't we?" By taking her attention away from the things that bothered her about him, appreciating and focusing on the things, she did like, her energy had shifted, and she started receiving more of the positive aspects of him. She changed her thinking pattern, and her relationship got better. Feel good and focus on the positives no matter what, and you will have a long-lasting relationship.

Anthea Morphitis

Feel Good and Watch What Happens

It's funny, as we only need ourselves to sort out anything and it all comes down to the way we feel, and our perspectives change that, and the evidence of your change of focus will shine through.

Trying to change another to satisfy your needs, holds the other to feel a lack of freedom. Just because we are in a relationship, it does not give anyone the right to hold the other hostage, trying to control what the other does. If your goal is to feel free, then allowing each other the freedom and support one another's dreams and desires, leave the guilt trips behind. Allowing them to be who they are and who they want to grow to be if it doesn't resonate with how you want your life to play out then that person is not for you, let go and keep it moving.

As I said we are forever expanding, therefore, even when we are aligned with our desires and receiving things we have asked for we are still going to want more, that's what we are here to experience.

We're better off enjoying the people in our lives, rather than moaning about them. If we don't like them, then walk away. Life is too short to spend our time being angry. We never know when a person is ready to leave this world, as I experienced myself recently.

Anthea Morphitis

Feel Good and Watch What Happens

Transition

The reason I am writing about transition is that I have just recently experienced what it feels like to have someone I love and care about pass away, so I thought I it would be a good idea to write and share my experienced.

I received a text yesterday from a good friend, asking me to call urgently!!

The second I read it, I felt there was something not right I picked up my phone and called her straight away, to be told the news that no one wants to hear: her mum had passed away. She had been diagnosed with cancer mid-December and passed away 23/1/13.

The last time I had experienced someone making their transition was 13 years ago, when my little cousin, aged 5, lost her fight and life to leukaemia.

It had been my mum's 60th birthday in December, and my friend's mum had joined us for a meal to celebrate. We had been to a fantastic Greek Restaurant where she had experienced a whole heap of different Greek dishes, and we all had lots of fun. I feel good knowing the last time I saw her she had the biggest smile on her face, with a beautiful full belly full of Greek food. As we sat outside at the end of our meal to smoke a cigarette together, we laughed and joked about us being the only ones wanting to smoke and how our bellies were ready to pop!

I wish there were some way of knowing this was going to be the last conversation we would ever have physically experienced together. I want to express my love to her and say thank you for being there for me on every step of my journey, your presence truly missed and you will remain in my heart and can honestly say I only have good memories of the times we spent together.

Anthea Morphitis

Feel Good and Watch What Happens

After sleeping on the news, I woke up refreshed, knowing that she was ready to go, and she was at total peace. It was her choice, and I genuinely believe she is now free of any pain and knows she is looking over me right now with a massive smile on her face and very proud.

I had spent two weeks before listening to Abraham Hicks on transition and not knowing why. I had never listened to anything about humans passing but just went with my intuition and I am glad I did as my friend's mum had been my friend too and a mum to me that I spoke about at the beginning of this book.

She was someone who had experienced significant parts of my journey with me. I met her when I was 11, and she took me under her wing, she was the most wonderful women on this planet; she was my birthing partner when my son was born, always had a door open for me. When I was locked out of my house as a teenager and had nowhere to stay, she welcomed me into her home with open arms and always had a bed for me.

It took my breath away as her daughter told me the news. I gasped for air and didn't know which way to turn; the emotion that went through my body was unexplainable.

I am glad I listened to my intuition and understood that we choose when we want to leave our bodies, and this understanding was incredibly soothing to me. Of course, I still went through the motions, knowing that I will never have the opportunity again to sit with her physically, and there would be no more physical interaction between us.

However, I know she is now everywhere, and I don't have to wait for her to answer the phone to speak to her. I now have access to her 24/7. I now know I can just focus and hear and feel her presence, and that's more than enough for me. I know when she is around, as I get goosebumps. It's amazing

Anthea Morphitis

Epilogue

Now we're coming to the end of my book, and you probably get the gist of my journey. I'm not the only one that has experienced some of my previous situations: family and friends experienced anger and pain alongside me, and have learnt how to be at peace with the past and let go.

However, there were many times that I wanted to give up, allowing the pressures of life get to me, feeling unworthy as a mother, feeling like a complete failure. Still, I didn't give up; I kept my faith by counting my blessings, learning to forgive myself and others, practising appreciation, reprograming my thoughts and feeling good. As a friend of mine says "Keep it moving." Don't allow circumstances to cloud your vision; you can this!

The past has gone; it's time to look forward and realise you can change the dynamics of your life with the vision of growth.

Believe me, as I know you know we are here to live life and become the person that we love and proud to show.

I stand here today with a different perspective on life, and I love me for who I am. I love the journey I have been on and love every second of my life thus far.

I continue to appreciate everything and everyone for who they are and eager of what's to come. I love where I stand, loving that I am inspired to write, inspiring others, and them inspiring me, loving the people that I am meeting and co-creating with.

Once you decide that the essential thing in life is to feel good, doors do open, and you will find yourself following your bliss.

Remember, Life will throw things your way. It's up to you how we choose to react and deal with the situation. Changing your thought process is like training at the gym; the results will not be visible after

Anthea Morphitis

Feel Good and Watch What Happens

one training session, you have to work at it if you want to see results. Feed your mind with positive thoughts daily. Think of yourself like a computer, needing updates regularly and a seed that needs nourishing to grow.

"You are in control of every thought and feeling that you experience: why not make your experience the best?"

Keep in mind everything you may be experiencing has a bigger purpose than your pain, its to build you not break you, to teach you to swim not drown you. Pain is growth and will take you past your comfort zone. You are the driver of your life, you can feed your mind with toxic thoughts, or you can feed your mind with heartwarming thoughts, the choice is yours, either way, your thoughts are your seeds and will grow the more you feed them, and the results of your seeds will manifest as your reality as part of the growth,

Take time to breathe, drink in the beauty of the world and appreciate whenever you can as those thoughts of appreciation are the seeds you want to grow.

"Never give up; life is what you make it!!"

Speak your future into existence, belief in where you want to go, if people around you don't believe in your dreams alongside you then they have got to go! Opinions are not facts, take them in and let them go. Surround yourself with the people who believe in you and encourage you to get up and go. You are capable of being anything you choose, remember to take the drivers wheel and decide where you want to go, although there may be bumps on the road you will reach your destination. Believe in possibilities. Believe in the road ahead. Enjoy your journey and the power you hold to Be, Do or Have anything you desire, and Life will go the best possible way that you didn't even know.

"Put your past to rest to re-create the best!!"

Anthea Morphitis

Feel Good and Watch What Happens

Feeling good and appreciating is part of those seeds for outstanding growth.

Writing this book has been so much fun and pushed me past my comfort zone. I have grown and learnt so much more since the start of it and had I not taken the driver's seat and been scared of my growth, then I know for sure you will not be reading this book, and I certainly would not grow in the way I have from expressing what I have pursued and got to know. I believed I could write a book and surrounded myself with the people who believed I could too, and this is the result of dreaming and believing in where you want to go.

I am sure that my children have their own story to there personal growth, having me as a mother and a friend. I hope I have done them proud, and they have enjoyed reading about my life from my perspective, and I hope it has helped them answer any questions that they may have held in their minds, of circumstances that they experienced with me. I embrace our journey together, and from here forth, I know it will continue to be a journey of fun, joy, prosperity, health, wealth and abundance.

I knew I would find what makes my juices flow, and I know if you haven't as yet you will, and I'd love to see you flourish and grow. I know I am a teacher, an up-lifter, a visionary. Teaching brings the best feeling to me. I love it; I love sharing my experiences and using my experiences to teach others, the fact that you can smooth those bumps in the road as I am living proof and I hope my children share what they know with other children to give them the perspective of natural growth. I believe that with time we will be free to teach this in schools and look forward to a newfound generation of children with a belief in their dreams and feel free to walk in the direction of what they believe and know.

While finishing this chapter, my daughter flagged up a point that I think would be good to share, she's looking for clarity, so I'm going to share.

Anthea Morphitis

Feel Good and Watch What Happens

The question is *"Mum, why are you writing a book about your past, when I've heard you say, to let go and let it rest?.*

Good point, right? The reason is that I am so at peace with my past that I can rethink and write everything down without getting upset. It has caused me to appreciate my life even more as I can see and recognise my growth how much my thought process has changed. I also want you, my readers, to know my journey and to connect with you at a different level, as you now know my lowest points and can now believe that you can live a better life no matter what you are facing right now. Without you knowing my journey, I could just be another person saying "I know how to change my life." My experiences will show you what I have been through, how I have come out the other end and how proud I stand today. I wanted to use myself as an example, especially to single parents, to shine a light on wellbeing; I am looking for the uplifting point in the people with whom I am interacting. I want to meet them at their most, allowing state and inspire them to their greater heights.

"Never give up; life is what you make it!!"

So, what I have I learnt and what do I know different now?

Play the game of life by making your thoughts playful and not so serious, choose to make the best of each situation, people circumstances and events, you have the choice to listen to others opinions of you and your life or not, negative or positive. You don't need anyone or anything such as cars, houses, clothes, etc. to define who you are, those things are part of the game of life and most importantly, your self-worth.

I hope me sharing the journey and my dedication of learning and understanding the Law of Attraction has helped you, the reader, with an understanding of who we are and help you with a new perspective of your life. I hope that sharing my journey can help you live the life you have always dreamt of, letting go of doubt and unworthiness and

Anthea Morphitis

being as happy as you possibly can be in each living moment. Knowing you are the director of your movie. You can choose to think whatever thoughts you want!

I wish you the best moving forward, and I know that all your dreams and desires will become your reality too. I would love to hear from you with any stories that you have to share about you, The Law of Attraction and your new-found life.

Thank you for having me be a part of your journey by reading 'Feel Good And Watch What Happens'. Much appreciation and love to you XXX

Remember, you are the creator of your life and where your attention goes the energy must flow and grow, so redirect your focus to where you know your life can prosper and start creating the joy you came to experience.

Love & Light

Anthea Morphitis

www.antheamorphitis.com

Aspire to inspire.

Anthea Morphitis

Feel Good and Watch What Happens

Anthea Morphitis

About The Author

Anthea Morphitis is passionate about life and dedicated to helping people feel as good as they can in each living moment. She believes we are the creators of our lives, and we attract to us what we are thinking and feeling 24/7.

She loves nothing more than to inspire and support people through the clarity of her example as a mother, friend, coach, writer and inspirational speaker, guiding each individual to connect with the 'Higher self' within. She shows people how to follow their intuition, by helping them harness the power of their thoughts and most importantly, their emotions. Allowing them to reach their full potential, creating lives they love and developing an enthusiasm for learning how to create what they would like to experience. She provides lessons that replace doubt and worry with expectation and knowledge of how to be happy and satisfied with where they stand in life right now, knowing that they will receive everything they want—and more. Her passion for helping others has guided her to her happiness as she now lives her dreams.

Anthea looks to uplift the people with whom she interacts by shining a light on their wellbeing, and she loves nothing more than to meet all individuals at their most allowing state and inspiring them to reach their greatest heights.

Her passion for helping others has served her well, and she loves being part of others' growth—this is her purpose in this lifetime.

Anthea Morphitis

Feel Good and Watch What Happens

Anthea is a single mother of two. Her bloodline is Greek Cypriot in origin; she was born and raised in North London. She now lives in Hertfordshire, where she runs her coaching practise that offers private consultation. Anthea is a Law of Attraction Specialist coach and offers her clients a life-changing breakthrough to happiness. She views everyone as having a purpose in life and having the potential to attract everything they have asked for. Anthea has confidence that anyone can live their dreams, and stands by the motto, "You Can Be, Do or Have anything". She holds that life is a true blessing and knows everyone has the potential to realize this blessing and live the life they have always dreamt of living. She believes the **BASIS** of life is **FREEDOM** and the **PURPOSE** of life is **JOY**!

Anthea Morphitis

www.ingramcontent.com/pod-product-compliance
Lightning Source LLC
Chambersburg PA
CBHW051948290426
44110CB00015B/2159